W9-BAE-081

3 1315 00458 9185

SEP   2007

DEMCO

THE RISE AND FALL OF THE SOVIET UNION

THE RISE AND FALL OF
THE SOVIET UNION

Other books in the
Opposing Viewpoints in World History series:

THE RISE AND FALL OF THE SOVIET UNION

Laurie Stoff, *Book Editor*

Bruce Glassman, *Vice President*
Bonnie Szumski, *Publisher*
Helen Cothran, *Managing Editor*

OPPOSING
VIEWPOINTS®
SERIES

GREENHAVEN PRESS
An imprint of Thomson Gale, a part of The Thomson Corporation

THOMSON

™

GALE

Detroit • New York • San Francisco • San Diego • New Haven, Conn.
Waterville, Maine • London • Munich

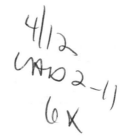

THOMSON

GALE

947.084 RIS

LIBRARY OF CONGRESS CATALOGING-IN-PUBLICATION DATA

The rise and fall of the Soviet Union / Laurie Stoff, book editor.
    p. cm. — (Opposing viewpoints in world history)
    Includes bibliographical references and index.
    ISBN 0-7377-2027-1 (lib. : alk. paper)
    1. Soviet Union—History. I. Stoff, Laurie. II. Series.
DK266.R547 2006
947.084—dc22
                                                2005045991

Printed in the United States of America

 # Contents

Chapter 2: What Foreign Policy Should the Soviets Pursue?

Chapter 3: How Did the Soviet Union Treat Its Citizens?

kinds of market mechanisms and a policy allowing open discussion of all aspects of Soviet life.

Foreword

On December 2, 1859, several hundred soldiers gathered at the outskirts of Charles Town, Virginia, to carry out, and provide security for, the execution of a shabbily dressed old man with a beard that hung to his chest. The execution of John Brown quickly became and has remained one of those pivotal historical events that are immersed in controversy. Some of Brown's contemporaries claimed that he was a religious fanatic who deserved to be executed for murder. Others claimed Brown was a heroic and selfless martyr whose execution was a tragedy. Historians have continued to debate which picture of Brown is closest to the truth.

The wildly diverging opinions on Brown arise from fundamental disputes involving slavery and race. In 1859 the United States was becoming increasingly polarized over the issue of slavery. Brown believed in both the necessity of violence to end slavery and in the full political and social equality of the races. This made him part of the radical fringe even in the North. Brown's conviction and execution stemmed from his role in leading twenty-one white and black followers to attack and occupy a federal weapons arsenal in Harpers Ferry, Virginia. Brown had hoped to ignite a large slave uprising. However, the raid begun on October 16, 1859, failed to draw support from local slaves; after less than thirty-six hours, Brown's forces were overrun by federal and local troops. Brown was wounded and captured, and ten of his followers were killed.

Brown's raid—and its intent to arm slaves and foment insurrection—was shocking to the South and much of the North. An editorial in the *Patriot*, an Albany, Georgia, newspaper, stated that Brown was a "notorious old thief and murderer" who deserved to be hanged. Many southerners expressed fears that Brown's actions were part of a broader northern conspiracy against the South—fears that seemed to be confirmed by captured letters documenting Brown's ties with some prominent northern abolitionists, some of whom had provided him with financial support. Such alarms also found confirmation in the pronouncements of some speakers such as writer Henry David Thoreau, who asserted that

Brown had "a perfect right to interfere by force with the slave-holder, in order to rescue the slave." But not all in the North defended Brown's actions. Abraham Lincoln and William Seward, leading politicians of the nascent Republican Party, both denounced Brown's raid. Abolitionists, including William Lloyd Garrison, called Brown's adventure "misguided, wild, and apparently insane." They were afraid Brown had done serious damage to the abolitionist cause.

Today, though all agree that Brown's ideas on racial equality are no longer radical, historical opinion remains divided on just what Brown thought he could accomplish with his raid, or even whether he was fully sane. Historian Russell Banks argues that even today opinions of Brown tend to split along racial lines. African Americans tend to view him as a hero, Banks argues, while whites are more likely to judge him mad. "And it's for the same reason—because he was a white man who was willing to sacrifice his life to liberate Black Americans. The very thing that makes him seem mad to white Americans is what makes him seem heroic to Black Americans."

The controversy over John Brown's life and death remind readers that history is replete with debate and controversy. Not only have major historical developments frequently been marked by fierce debates as they happened, but historians examining the same events in retrospect have often come to opposite conclusions about their causes, effects, and significance. By featuring both contemporaneous and retrospective disputes over historical events in a pro/con format, the Opposing Viewpoints in World History series can help readers gain a deeper understanding of important historical issues, see how historical judgments unfold, and develop critical thinking skills. Each article is preceded by a concise summary of its main ideas and information about the author. An in-depth book introduction and prefaces to each chapter provide background and context. An annotated table of contents and index help readers quickly locate material of interest. Each book also features an extensive bibliography for further research, questions designed to spark discussion and promote close reading and critical thinking, and a chronology of events.

 **Introduction**

The Great Experiment

The history of the Soviet Union is relatively short in comparison with the histories of the other nations of the world: little more than seventy years long. Despite its brevity, it is replete with controversy, dramatic events, tragedy, and immense historical significance. Perhaps most significantly, the Soviet Union is considered one of the greatest social experiments of modern civilization. The collapse of the USSR in 1991 has been interpreted by many as the ultimate failure of Soviet communism and a vindication for those who claim the system was a bane on humanity. Yet one cannot deny the Soviet Union's tremendous impact on the world. It was the first attempt to build a Communist society, and although it never approximated the egalitarian utopia its ideology espoused, it fundamentally changed life in Russia and the other Soviet republics. Moreover, the Soviet Union became a modern, industrial nation and achieved global superpower status. The establishment of Soviet power in 1917 was just the beginning of this experiment. Throughout its history the leaders of the Soviet Union amended and adjusted the system in an effort to make it work. The country was constantly undergoing changes and reforms, while also remaining the same in many ways. In fact, it can be argued that it was this experimental nature that both allowed it to survive as long as it did and ultimately led to its demise when it tried to change too much.

The Russian Revolution of 1917 may have shocked other parts of the world, but in Russia the momentum toward such political upheaval had been steadily building throughout much of the nineteenth century. The revolutionaries were appalled by the conditions in which the majority of their countrymen were forced to live. While a very small portion of the population lived in opulent wealth and decadent luxury, more than 90 percent barely eked out their subsistence. Politically, the citizens of prerevolutionary Russia had little freedom. The autocratic government persecuted those who spoke out against the injustices of the system. Political participation was virtually nonexistent until 1905, and even then it was severely restricted. Minority populations living within the Russian Empire were subjected to intense discrimination and even violence. Moreover, the system was proving to be increasingly ineffective and even destructive. Russia, once a great world power, was losing its prowess and its influence. Russia entered the First World War with one of the largest armies in the world, but it proved to be poorly run and incapable of standing up to the military machines of its enemies. By 1917 the majority of Russians were no longer willing to support the monarchy, and in February they overturned the czar, ending hundreds of years of autocratic rule.

Initially, those who took control after the czar abdicated his throne in 1917 favored establishing a representative democracy similar to Great Britain. They set up a provisional government to rule until a constituent assembly could be called and elections for a legislature could be held. But many advocated a Socialist system in which there would be equality for all citizens and in which all would cooperate for the good of the whole. They were, by and large, followers of Karl Marx, who had outlined a theory of history based on stages. Marx maintained that the current stage of history in the West was that of bourgeois capitalism, wherein the middle class controlled business and industry and exploited the workers by paying them low salaries and keeping most of the profits. Their economic power gave them political power, and therefore the governments of the West were largely controlled by the bourgeoisie. In Russia, however, this phase had not really taken shape, since the country was still controlled by and large by the landholding aristocracy. Many Russian Marxists, therefore, interpreted the February Revolution as the "bourgeois" revolution, which would establish capitalism and middle-class political control. For them, it was necessary to wait for this stage of history to develop sufficiently before moving on to the next stage of socialism, the last and inevitable stage according to Marx.

Other Russian Marxists argued that Russia had already been experiencing bourgeois capitalism, and that now was the time for the Socialist revolution. This view was promoted especially by Vladimir I. Lenin, head of the Bolshevik wing of the Russian Social Democratic Labor Party. Lenin insisted that Russian revolutionaries could not sit by idly while "history develops" and let the suffering of millions of people continue. Therefore, he and his party began to plan for a second revolution in which they would seize control of the organs of government. They carried out this revolution in November (October according to the old Russian calendar)[1] and overturned the weak provisional government.

Although the Bolsheviks managed to take control of the government in the capital, Petrograd,[2] many people opposed their rule. In the summer of 1918 the country erupted in civil war, as the opponents of the Bolsheviks fought to oust them from power. The civil war lasted for three years, but it was not just a military effort. The Bolsheviks were also fighting a political and social war to convince the people of Russia that socialism was the best system for them. They introduced an all-out propaganda effort meant to demonstrate the benefits of socialism and the progress it would bring. They brought electricity to the peasants, showed them movies, and made automobiles, airplanes, and other modern technological advances available to them. To combat their political enemies, the Bolsheviks created a political police force, the Cheka, despite the fact that many of their own ranks had suffered at the hands of the czarist political police, the Okhrana. The Cheka went through a number of transformations over the years of Soviet rule until it became the KGB (secret police), but its functions remained largely the same: to root out "enemies of the people."

Building a New Society

Even before achieving victory in the civil war, Lenin and the other original architects of the Soviet system set out to build a brand-new kind of society. The old society had largely collapsed, and whatever remnants remained, the new leaders were determined to

1. The Bolsheviks changed the Russian calendar to match the one used in the West, which was thirteen days ahead of the old Russian calendar.   2. St. Petersburg before the onset of World War I, when the name was changed to Petrograd because of anti-German sentiment

destroy. They had a theoretical basis for this new system, envisioning a classless society without exploitation, with equality of all citizens, with communal ownership of industry and enterprise. However, they had no blueprint telling them how to proceed with its construction. Marx had given them an ideology, but not the details of how to achieve it. Therefore, the Soviet leaders carried out a great deal of experimentation. They also ended up using elements of the old system, whether consciously or not. While they continued to believe wholly in the ideology, they used a variety of interpretations of Marxism, which allowed much flexibility in attempting to remake Russia. Within the party there was a great deal of debate on how to proceed with this task, and the arguments were often bitter.

The first task the new Soviet leaders were faced with was rebuilding the Russian economy, which was devastated as a result of the world war and massive mismanagement. During the civil war Lenin introduced a policy called War Communism in order to cope with the chaos. This policy included nationalization of banking, transportation, foreign trade, and large-scale industry. As a result, the state controlled most of the economy. The state also rationed goods and services and forcibly collected food and grain from the peasants in the countryside in order to feed the workers in the cities. The government enjoined peasants to leave their homesteads and join kolkhozy, or collective farms. When its will was not carried out, the state used force against the population. The Soviet leadership justified these efforts on the grounds that they prevented the total collapse of the economy and shored up the power of the new regime. Moreover, they were deemed necessary in the attempt to transform the socioeconomic structure from capitalist to Communist.

By the end of the civil war in 1921, it had become clear that War Communism was not succeeding. There was widespread resistance to forced grain seizures and to joining collective farms. Starving peasants poured into the cities searching for food. The railway system, now run by the government, was largely in ruin; as a result, factories had difficulty receiving the raw materials necessary for production. Labor productivity decreased dramatically. Fuel shortages plagued the larger cities. To aggravate the problems of War Communism, a terrible drought hit the country and a famine ensued. Once the civil war was over and the Communist Party (the new name for the Bolshevik Party) firmly was in power, it was decided to abandon the policies of War Communism. Most Soviet leaders realized that they could not impose communism overnight, and that slower, more transitional measures would be necessary.

Lenin now proposed the New Economic Policy (NEP), which sought to reintroduce some elements of the market, including private enterprise and ownership, in order to allow the economy to recover. Although some Marxists were uncomfortable with what seemed to be a retreat to capitalism, the Soviet leadership believed this step was necessary to create the conditions for future progress toward socialism. The programs of the NEP managed to help the economy recover from the devastation of the war years. The 1920s was probably the most experimental decade in Soviet history, as the Communists implemented numerous policies and programs in an effort to solve the problems they faced. Debates on policy and the nature of the revolution were allowed within the party and were conducted frequently. Some degree of freedom of expression was tolerated in literature and the arts. New ideas about the structure of society and family life were introduced. Divorce and abortion were legalized and made widely accessible. Women were provided a great deal of opportunity and were encouraged to work outside the home, with the state providing child care. The relative freedom and experimentation of the 1920s were tempered, however. It was also during this time that the Communist Party, the sole political party allowed to function, began to monopolize all aspects of political life, even dictating social policy. The secret police expanded its operation, censorship was increased, and the party began dictating what the role of art and literature should be in Socialist society.

The Stalin Years

When Lenin died in 1924 a triumvirate of Lev Kamenev, Grigori Zinoviev, and Joseph Stalin ruled the Soviet Union. Leon Trotsky, an instrumental figure during the revolution, also continued to be an extremely important and powerful leader in the Soviet government. He and Stalin soon became embroiled in a power struggle for leadership of the party and the state, and Stalin eventually emerged the sole ruler. Once he had consolidated his power, Stalin began to introduce his own vision of "revolution." Stalin's first steps were economic. The NEP had managed to restore the Soviet economy, but many Communists were uneasy with its heavy reliance on capitalism. To them it was an internal contradiction to build socialism using capitalist measures. Stalin's policies resolved this contradiction. He ended the NEP and introduced a highly centralized state-run economic strategy that eliminated private enterprise. To this end he implemented a series of five-year plans that directed all aspects of economic production. His top priority was industrialization. The building of socialism was always understood to include massive industrialization and modernization. For Stalin, socialism was the best way to bring progress and allow Russia to become a powerful industrial state. This meant transforming a largely agrarian society of rural peasants into an industrial society of urban workers. Thus, he laid a course of fast-paced forced industrialization at all costs, including forced labor. In the process, thousands died due to the harsh conditions of labor imposed upon them.

In addition to forced industrialization, Stalin introduced mass collectivization of agriculture. He required peasants to leave individual farms and join state-owned and -run kolkhozy. Those who opposed this policy were labeled "kulaks" (rich peasants) and systematically divested of their land, arrested, sent to Siberian labor camps, or executed. Like industrial production, agriculture was now to be directed and planned by the state. Centralized planning, however, proved ill equipped to handle agricultural production. The result was tremendous shortages, complicated by famines, and thus the starvation of millions of Soviet citizens.

Although Stalin's changes in economic policy were implemented in an attempt to bring the Soviet Union closer to socialism, they were not helping to create an egalitarian society. In fact, he had no intention of doing so. For Stalin, socialism was a means by which the Soviet Union could achieve the modernization and technological advancement necessary to build a powerful military machine and become a leader among the industrialized nations.

He moved to further restrict the rights and even movements of the Soviet citizens. In a measure reminiscent of czarist days, he reintroduced the system of passport identification required for movement within as well as outside the country. Instead of promoting internationalism and cooperation between the working classes of all countries, as Marx had preached, he championed the greatness of Russia. Although Stalin himself was from the nation of Georgia in Caucasia, he possessed a strong streak of Russian chauvinism.

In fact, most of the egalitarian aspects of socialism were trampled upon under Stalin. He purged the party, and society, of the old revolutionary intelligentsia, executing them after conducting "show trials" backed by coerced false confessions of treasonous behavior. Persecution and mass deportations of non-Russians took place under his rule. Women lost much of the ground they had achieved in the 1920s. He rescinded the legality of abortion, made divorce difficult for women to obtain, and imposed a new family code that stressed traditional values and conventional motherhood over professional achievement for women. Stalin also moved to end the experimentation with and openness to different ideas that had flowered during the 1920s.

There are those who argue that the nature of Russian Marxism contained all the elements that eventually manifested themselves in Stalinism. The violence and terror, the Russian nationalism, the lack of true egalitarianism, and the authoritarianism could all be found in Lenin's policies. Therefore, they argue, communism in the Soviet Union would have developed along similar lines with or without the personality of Stalin. Others maintain that Stalinism represents a break with the Marxism of Lenin and his cohorts and that Stalin truly abandoned the ideology of his predecessors. Yet it is undeniable that Stalin's system fundamentally changed life in the Soviet Union. His policies required mass mobilization and tremendous sacrifice of the population and seemingly boundless tyranny. After Stalin's death the system could not be maintained, and it was obvious that most Soviets did not desire it to continue. When Nikita Khrushchev ascended to power in 1954, the nation was ripe for change yet again, and the new leader set about to satisfy this drive.

The Post-Stalin "Thaw"

Khrushchev was a committed Marxist who believed firmly that its ideology was the best system for Russia and the best way for Russia to be a great power. Therefore, he worked to undo the greatest damages caused by the excesses of Stalinism while remaining true to the goal of achieving communism. His secret speech to the Twentieth Party Congress condemned Stalin for his crimes but simultaneously commended him for being a great leader. Khrushchev began the process of de-Stalinization by releasing political prisoners from the gulags, or labor camps. Eventually, millions of people were freed from the gulags. Thousands of those falsely accused by Stalin were rehabilitated. He began to allow some degree of cultural freedom, opening the door to greater artistic and literary expression. He changed economic policy radically by shifting authority away from the center to locally controlled economic councils (*sovnarkhozy*). He changed Soviet foreign policy from one of constant vigilance against the capitalist world with which war was seen as inevitable to one of "peaceful coexistence."

There were, however, many elements of the Stalinist system that were retained both because they had become so deeply institutionalized and because the Soviet leadership continued to believe in their usefulness. The "thaw" in culture allowing greater freedom of expression was closely monitored by the ever-watchful state, and censorship still dictated what was published and what was banned. Indoctrination and propaganda continued to be hallmarks of the Soviet state. The KGB continued to function despite having its powers reduced. The policy of "peaceful coexistence" was adopted largely as a practical measure, the result of difficulties in keeping up with the West in the arms race. Despite his rhetoric of peace, Khrushchev remained convinced that the Soviet Union would surpass the West and that communism would be victorious throughout the world. On several occasions, the most dramatic of which was the Cuban missile crisis, he expressed extreme bravado in foreign policy, as if he was daring the West to go to war with the Soviet Union. The push for technological modernization continued, but without the mass mobilization and coercion of the Stalinist period. Indeed, under Khrushchev, the Soviet Union achieved great feats, such as launching the world's first space satellite, *Sputnik*, in 1957, and four years later sending the first man into space.

Although Khrushchev was a committed Communist, the majority of the party could not tolerate the risky nature of his reforms. He was unceremoniously ousted in 1964, but the fact that he was not killed after being deposed signifies the great change his rule had brought to Soviet society after the violence of the Stalin era. Those who assumed the mantle of power after him were much more conservative. The period under Khrushchev's successor, Leonid Brezhnev, is often portrayed as one of stagnation. Compared with the dramatic and energetic leadership of those who came before him, Brezhnev appears dull and his tenure remarkably stable. He was very conservative and deeply suspicious of liberalization. Therefore, he and his administration made no attempts at bold reform, despite the problems facing the Soviet Union. They did, however, continue to tinker, to make small-scale changes they hoped would improve the functioning of the system. This was particularly so in economic matters, where the Soviet Union was clearly lagging.

Perhaps the most dramatic change that occurred during the Brezhnev years was the open admission by the leadership that socialism would not provide the Soviet population with the utopia of a just and affluent society as promised by Marxist ideology. Instead, they announced that they had achieved socialism, and, as historian Peter Kenez contends, "the implication was that constant experimentation . . . would largely be abandoned."[3] Not only did the Soviet leadership give up the goal of equality, they allowed inequalities to flourish, as the top echelon of society—a political elite known as the *nomenklatura*—had access to goods and services the rest of the population was denied. They had the best homes and automobiles, an abundance of the best foods, and some were even allowed to travel to the West. The Brezhnev period was also characterized by a significant increase in corruption within the government. The huge bureaucracy became almost unmanageable, and bribes were often the only way people could get anything accomplished.

---

3. Peter Kenez, *A History of the Soviet Union from the Beginning to the End.* Cambridge: Cambridge University Press, 1999, p. 216.

Although the Soviet economy had achieved enough stability to allow most Soviet citizens to satisfy their basic needs, it came to stagnate under Brezhnev. Despite attempts at moderate reform, the leadership could not get the economy to improve or to provide greater availability of food and consumer goods. Wages continued to rise, but the standard of living remained constant because people had very little to spend their money on. As a result, a black market, or second economy, flourished and was unofficially tolerated by the regime. General dissatisfaction also increased, especially as Soviet citizens became aware of the disparities between life in the West and that in the Communist East.

One of the most important developments of the Brezhnev era was the rise of dissent. Dissent in the Soviet Union had actually begun under Khrushchev, once the totalitarianism of Stalin was ended and there was some degree of freedom of expression granted during the "thaw." People found it increasingly acceptable to speak critically of the regime, and Khrushchev tolerated this criticism to an extent. Brezhnev, however, attempted to repress dissent. The Soviet leadership remained deathly frightened of openness and the free flow of information. They had seen what had happened in Eastern Europe, when Poles and Hungarians attempted to carry out revolutions against the Communists while Khrushchev was in power. Khrushchev had used force to end the Hungarian Revolution in 1956, and when a similar situation unfolded in Czechoslovakia in 1968, Brezhnev did not hesitate to do the same. Within the Soviet Union, the KGB was used to try to stop dissent. But without using violent force, this goal was nearly impossible to accomplish. Dissidents used underground publications and sneaked their works out of the country to be published in the West. Arrests were made, trials were held, and those found guilty were imprisoned or exiled. However, in the process those convicted immediately became martyrs, which made them more powerful. When the writers Iulii Daniel and Andrei Siniavskii were arrested and tried for spreading "anti-Soviet propaganda," news of the trial encouraged others to speak out and organize their efforts. In this sense, the regime's actions backfired. Instead of scaring people into submission, it caused the dissident movement to grow and spread.

In addition to being intolerant of dissent, the Brezhnev regime looked unfavorably upon nationalist movements in the non-Russian republics. Since their incorporation into the USSR, most nationalities had been encouraged, sometimes forcibly, to abandon their national aspirations and identities and become cosmopolitan Soviets. This often meant that the use of their native languages was suppressed (Russian was the official language of the Soviet Union), and manifestation of their religion and culture were highly discouraged, again, sometimes forcibly. Under Stalin, terror was used in an attempt to make the Soviet Union as culturally uniform as possible. After his death and the end of terror, nationalism began to resurface. The leadership in Moscow attempted to curb expressions of nationalism without the use of the excessive force that characterized the Stalin era. At the same time, Stalin's successors were challenged by movements in Eastern Europe that demanded greater autonomy in internal policy. Both Khrushchev and Brezhnev had no qualms about using force to suppress these challenges. None of their tactics proved effective, however, and nationalist sentiment both within the Soviet Union and without continued to grow. Eventually, the pressure of nationalism would be one of the major factors contributing to the collapse of the USSR.

By the end of the Brezhnev era, the Soviet Union had become a superpower in the world based on its military strength, but at home its economy and political system were troubled. When Brezhnev died in 1982 he was replaced by Yuri Andropov, who retained his conservatism and continued his policies in most areas. Although he saw no need for large-scale changes, he was seen by some as a reformer. He died only a year and half later, however, before he was able to institute any significant policy. Konstantin Chernenko succeeded Andropov, but his short rule was punctuated by illness, and he failed to make any significant contribution to Soviet government. When he died in 1985, his second in command, Mikhail Gorbachev, took the helm. Gorbachev was comparatively young, extremely dynamic, and intent upon reforming a system he saw as severely ailing.

Drastic Reform Under Gorbachev

There are many who identify Gorbachev as the most thorough reformer of Soviet history. That being largely true, it must be ac-

knowledged that without the changes implemented by Khrushchev, Gorbachev most likely would never have been able to introduce his reforms. Yet Gorbachev was willing to take his reforms
farther than Khrushchev had been willing to do during his rule.
One of the first things he did upon assuming power was to introduce an antialcohol campaign. Alcoholism caused many problems
in Soviet society, including low productivity, disease, death, and
crime. His efforts did manage to reduce alcohol consumption, but
the policy was extremely unpopular, cut into state revenues from
the sale of vodka, and spurred moonshining. He instituted a "new
course" in foreign policy in an effort to improve relations with the
West, particularly with the United States. He reduced military
spending and removed Soviet influence from remote places in an
effort to reserve much-needed spending for the domestic economy and to demonstrate his commitment to peace.

Gorbachev's primary concerns were with domestic policy, especially the weak economy. Therefore, his most sweeping changes
were introduced in this area. He proposed a drastic perestroika,
or restructuring of the economy, the political system, and Soviet
life in general. Yet his reforms had only modest results, and in an
effort to accelerate the pace of change and make his reforms more
effective, Gorbachev introduced glasnost, or openness, allowing
the free flow of information and freedom of expression. He implemented what he termed "market socialism," which aimed at
scaling back state ownership of major industries, infusing the system with some limited privatization and a simulated market, a
market introduced and largely controlled by the state. These
changes were, in fact, very reminiscent of the policies of the NEP
utilized in the 1920s to revive the ailing economy. He tried to democratize the political system, while still retaining the essential elements of socialism.

In the end, these efforts started a process of liberalization that
effectively could not be stopped. When it became clear that his
measures were not improving the economy, the Soviet people lost
patience with him and the party. They blamed most of the country's problems on them and thus communism, which was increasingly losing its credibility as a viable system. This outcome, cou-
pled with the rise of nationalist sentiment, eventually led to the

disintegration of the USSR. Gorbachev had tried to change the system in order to preserve it, but the majority of people wanted to eradicate the system itself. They did not feel it was worth preserving, for it was the cause of their problems. The result was the demise of the Soviet system.

Many questions and controversies continue to surround this dramatic event. Much of the world was shocked by the collapse of the USSR, which theretofore had been perceived as a remarkably stable entity. Many saw the collapse as the result of a democratic movement among the peoples of the Soviet Union. But there are others, including many Communists themselves, who saw the opportunities that ending communism and transitioning to capitalism would bring, particularly for improving their finances. In the end, for most the Soviet Communist system had become bankrupt and had lost its legitimacy. When the opportunity for change presented itself, they took it.

The change from a Communist system was, and continues to be, extremely difficult. The dismantling of the Soviet Union left much chaos and confusion. Freedom and capitalism were often interpreted as license to do just about anything. The rule of law had to be reestablished, but many were unsure just what the law was. The social safety net provided by the Soviet government and the stability maintained by the centrally planned economy disappeared almost overnight. The concepts of a free market and private business were foreign to most people, and they did not know quite how to proceed. Institutions and methods of the Soviet period did not disappear overnight; in many cases they remained in place, as they were the only ones people understood. The KGB became the FSB (Federal Security Service), but its function and form was not greatly altered. Moreover, although the Communists were no longer in power, control of the government was not merely transferred from the hands of former Communists to liberal reformers and democrats. Rather, power more often remained in the hands of old Communists who took on new labels. The countries of the former Soviet Union continue to struggle with their new forms in the hope of providing a better future for their citizens.

CHAPTER 1

Should the Russian Monarchy Be Overthrown?

# Chapter Preface

For hundreds of years Russia was ruled as a czarist autocracy—with all power in the hands of the monarch. Citizens of the Russian Empire were not able to participate in the political affairs of their country. In 1905, after a bloody uprising, Czar Nicholas II reluctantly agreed to convene a constitutional assembly. The powers of this assembly, called the Duma, were relatively weak, however, and the czar retained almost absolute control. Many Russians strongly opposed the heavy-handed and often oppressive policies of the monarchy. The opposition was composed of various groups with different ideas about what kind of government Russia should have. These groups included revolutionaries who wanted to overturn the entire czarist system, as well as reformers, who merely wanted to make it more democratic. Some were Communists, some were Socialists, while others were constitutional democrats. The disagreements among these groups often became violent.

The opposition to czarism ultimately came to a head during the First World War. Russia was suffering from devastating economic difficulties and was losing the war. Many blamed the czar, his advisers, and his ministers for grossly mismanaging the nation during this time. The frustration with these wartime problems together with hundreds of years of poverty and oppression finally culminated in a revolution in February 1917. The czar and his government were overthrown and a constitutional democracy was installed. Yet this outcome did not satisfy all of Russia's citizens, particularly the revolutionary Communists and Socialists. They believed that the liberal democratic government only had the interests of the wealthy and middle classes in mind and would do little to alleviate the poverty and suffering of the peasants and the working classes, who made up the majority of Russian citizens. These groups believed that the best type of government for Russia was one in which the lower classes held political and economic control. One of the main groups in favor of this idea was the Russian Social Democratic Labor Party which included two subgroups known as the Bolsheviks and Mensheviks.

While the revolutionaries tended to agree on the best form of government, they disagreed regarding when and how the revolution should occur. Most adhered to the tenets of Socialist theorist Karl Marx, who had argued that working-class leadership would come only when Russia reached a certain stage of historical development.

According to Marx, communism could only be achieved when a country had completed its capitalist stage of development. In other words, a country had to have a fully developed capitalist system, complete with industrialization and rule by the middle class. Then, Marx maintained, the working class could revolt against its oppressive leaders and take control. But Russia had only just begun to obtain the trappings of capitalism and had just started to industrial-

Karl Marx

ize. Therefore, many Bolsheviks, as well as other Socialists, argued that they had to wait for their revolution. Others, such as Vladimir I. Lenin, who became the leader of the Bolsheviks and eventually of the Soviet Union, argued that Russia's circumstances were unique and that it would be irresponsible of the Socialists to ignore the suffering of the masses by waiting to stage a revolution.

Ultimately, Lenin won this argument, and the Bolsheviks began preparing for action. When none of the other political parties were willing to take action, Lenin and his party made bold promises. They launched their revolution on October 25, 1917.[1] The Bolsheviks seized all the key government institutions in the capital, Petrograd (previously called St. Petersburg). They captured Moscow as well, and then city after city fell to Bolshevik control.

There is much debate about whether the majority of the Russian people actually backed the Bolsheviks. Some believe the Bol-

1. Before 1918 the Russians used the Julian calendar, which was thirteen days behind the Gregorian calendar used in the West. In the West, the date was November 7.

sheviks merely carried out a coup d'état when their small group ousted the equally small government. Others maintain that the people responded to the Bolsheviks' slogan "Peace, Bread, and Land," which was extremely popular among the masses of war-weary, hungry, and poor Russian people. One thing is clear, however: most Russians were peasants who lived in the countryside and had little understanding of politics and revolutionary ideas. For them, ending the war and feeding their children were the most important goals. While traditionally they had expressed much loyalty to the czar, they were most focused on these practical matters. Whether they wanted or even comprehended a Socialist government is another matter altogether.

Viewpoint 1

"Only firm Tsarist authority ... can provide unconditional guarantees for a durable legal order in such a multi-national state as Russia."

The Monarchy Should Be Retained

Union of the Russian People

In 1905, in response to widespread discontent and a general strike that crippled Russia's economy, Czar Nicholas II issued the October Manifesto. This document convened the first representative legislative assembly in Russia, legalized political parties, and guaranteed certain civil rights. With this newfound freedom of activity, Russian citizens formed a wide variety of political associations, advocating an equally vast array of political programs. The Union of the Russian People, formed in 1905, was a staunchly conservative, pro-czarist, and fervently religious (Orthodox) party, as represented by the slogan "Autocracy, Nationality, and Orthodoxy." In this viewpoint, which is a segment of its political program issued in 1905, the group expresses the idea that Russia must remain a monarchy, as the czar is the main pillar of Russian life. The leaders of the union maintain that the czar was ordained by God to be the ruler of Russia and his benevolent rule is what makes Russia great. Their program promotes a nationalist agenda that strongly favors ethnic Russians over others (Russia was a multinational and multiethnic em-

Union of the Russian People, "Program of the Union of the Russian People, 1905," *Imperial Russia: A Sourcebook, 1700–1917*, edited by Basil Dmytryshyn. Hinsdale, IL: The Dryden Press, 1974.

pire) and seeks to restrict the rights of non-Russians, particularly Jews. The union also argues that the multinational nature of the Russian state demands an autocratic system of government to maintain law and order. The group concludes that Russian Orthodoxy is the only religion appropriate for the Russian nation and is similarly an essential aspect of Russian life and governance.

Russian People!
The great manifesto of October 30 [manifesto issued by Tsar Nicholas II establishing constitutional government] granted us civil freedom on the basis of inviolability of person, freedom of expression, conscience, meetings and unions. In spite of this Tsarist grace, under the cover of promised freedom, many of us in fact have joined the darkest slavery of a mysterious, unknown, coarse, and all-destructive force which arbitrarily determines our fate without any legal authority, issues its own "manifestoes" and openly advocates a whole series of impractical demands, such as complete destruction of the Russian army and its replacement by militia subordinate to city administration, organization of a social democratic republic, and so forth. The enemies of the Tsar and of the country, by means of deception, threats, and violence, cause strikes in factories and mills, stop trains, disrupt trade, inflict tremendous loss to the entire state, and deprive hundreds of thousands of poor people of work in order to force them into violence through hunger. Our children are deprived of the possibility of education, the sick are dying, not being able to obtain medicine. . . . The trouble has not stopped in spite of the fact that we have received freedom, the same "freedom" which everyone has demanded so ardently. God only knows how far this anarchy will lead. One thing, however, is certain: we are proceeding directly to the downfall and destruction of the Russian state. This is why we call upon all those honest Russian people, irrespective of their profession or status, who are loyal to the Tsar, the country, and traditional Russian principles, to unite in order to conduct an active struggle by every legal means against arbitrariness, violence, and other repulsive manifestations of the recently granted freedom.

Foundations

The ultimate aim which this Union of the Russian People must seek is the introduction of a firm, durable, legal order, on the basis of the following foundations:

1. Unity and indivisibility of the Russian Empire and stability of the basic foundations of Russian statehood, because only firm Tsarist authority, based on a direct union between the Tsar and the people, or their elected representatives, can provide unconditional guarantees for a durable legal order in such a multi-national state as Russia.

2. Establishment of a State Duma with the right to report directly to the Sovereign, the right to address an inquiry to the ministers, the right to control the activity of the ministers, and the right to petition the Emperor that the former be dismissed and tried in the courts.

3. Coordination of the activity of ministers and establishment of their firm, actual responsibility, similar to the responsibility of all other officials, for every irregularity connected with their service and for damages suffered by private individuals, including bringing them to the attention of the Procurator.

4. Allowing the election of Jews to the State Duma, not more than three persons, elected by the entire Jewish population of the Russian Empire to present in the Duma the special needs of the Jewish population. Such limitation is necessary because of the disruptive, anti-state activity of the united Jewish masses, their unceasing hatred of everything Russian, and the unscrupulousness which they so openly demonstrated during the recent revolutionary movement.

5. The realization of freedom and inviolability granted by the Manifesto of October 30; that is, protection of individuals from the arbitrariness and violence of officials, of private individuals as well as of all sorts of societies, unions, and committees, both open and secret.

6. Establishment of a firm criminal responsibility of the press to protect the basic foundation of the state system, based on special legislation similar to that which exists in the countries of Western Europe.

7. Firm, severe, and actual protection of property rights of private individuals, of societies, and of the state.

The basis of our Union is brotherly love towards neighbors, and we therefore do not allow any of the arbitrariness, force, falsehoods, rumors, distortions, secret or similar means of struggle used by our enemies, by the Tsar's enemies, or by enemies of the country.

The Statute of the Union of the Russian People

I. *The Aim of the Union* 1. The Union of the Russian People sets as its undeviating goal a durable unity of the Russian people of all classes and professions to work for the general good of our fatherland—a Russia united and indivisible.

II. *Program* 2. The well being of the country should consist of a firm preservation of Russian autocracy, orthodoxy, and nationality, and of the establishment of a State Duma, order, and legality.

3. Russian autocracy was created by national wisdom, sanctified by the Church, and justified by history. Our autocracy consists of unity between the Tsar and the people.

Note: Convinced that national well being consists of the unity between the Russian Tsar and the people, the Union acknowledges that the present ministerial bureaucratic system, which separates the pure soul of the Russian Tsar from the people, and which has appropriated a number of rights that truly belong to the Russian autocratic power, has brought our country to grave troubles and should therefore be changed fundamentally. At the same time the Union firmly believes that a change of the existing order should be accomplished not through the introduction of certain restrictive institutions such as constitutional or constituent assemblies, but rather through convocation of a State Duma as an institution which would represent a direct tie between the autocratic will of the Tsar and the right of the people.

4. The Russian people are Orthodox people and therefore the Orthodox faith remains steadfastly the official religion of the Russian Empire. All subjects of the Empire, however, have the freedom of religious worship.

5. The Russian nation, as the gatherer of Russian lands and the

creator of the great might of the state, enjoys a preferential position in national life and in national administration.

Note: All institutions of the Russian state should be united and should constantly strive to maintain the greatness of Russia and the preferential rights of the Russian nation that legally belong to them, so that the numerous minorities that inhabit our country would consider it their privilege to be a part of the Russian Empire and would not consider themselves oppressed.

Note: The Russian language is and should be the official language of the Russian Empire for all of its people.

6. The State Duma, the bulwark of autocracy, should not demand any limitations on the supreme authority of the Tsar. It should only inform him of the real needs of the people and of the state and help the Lawgiver to realize the necessary reforms.

7. The immediate activity of authorities should be directed toward the introduction of a firm order and legality guaranteeing freedom of speech, press, assembly, and unions, and the inviolability of the individual. There should be established a rule that would determine the limits of these freedoms in order to prevent the violation of the established system, the endangering of the rights of other individuals, and thus to protect freedom itself.

Viewpoint 2

"The most outstanding among [the] relics of the past, the mightiest bulwark of . . . barbarism, is the tsarist autocracy."

The Monarchy Should Be Overthrown in Russia

Russian Social Democratic Labor Party (Bolsheviks)

Prior to 1905 political organization was illegal in Russia, as was open discussion of political aspirations or opposition to the czarist government. But opposition existed nonetheless, and since the mid-1800s it had been fomenting in Russia in response to the autocratic policies of the monarchy. Many of these oppositionists advocated a revolutionary overthrow of the czar's government. The Russian Social Democratic Labor Party (RSDLP) was one such group. Formed in the last years of the nineteenth century, the party consisted of followers of Karl Marx, who advocated a system of economic and social equality based on communal labor. The leaders of the RSDLP were forced to live abroad or risk imprisonment in Russia. In 1903 the party split into two competing factions, the Bolsheviks (which means majority, although this was actually the smaller of the two groups) and the Mensheviks (which means minority). The main difference between the two

Russian Social Democratic Labor Party, "Program of the Russian Social Democratic Labor Party (Bolsheviks)," *Resolutions and Decisions of the Communist Party of the Soviet Union, vol. 1: The Russian Social Democratic Labour Party, 1898–October 1917*, edited by R.C. Elwood. Toronto: University of Toronto Press, 1974.

35

groups was that the Bolsheviks, led by Vladimir I. Lenin, advocated an immediate revolution to end the oppression of autocracy in Russia and establish a socialist state. The Mensheviks, on the other hand, believed Russia was not ready for socialism and had to develop a capitalist economy first. In this viewpoint the Bolsheviks outline their political program, to be implemented after the revolution has been accomplished. The monarchy, according to the Bolsheviks, is a barbaric institution that is hostile to its own subjects and forces them to live in chains. Therefore, it should be dismantled and replaced with a socialist system. The Bolsheviks' main goals are to secure citizens' and workers' freedoms, while protecting them from unduly harsh labor practices.

In Russia, where capitalism has already become the dominant mode of production, there are still preserved numerous vestiges of the old pre-capitalist order, when the toiling masses were serfs of the landowners, the state, or the sovereign. Greatly hampering economic progress, these vestiges interfere with the many-sided development of the class struggle of the proletariat, help to preserve and strengthen the most barbarous forms of exploitation by the state and the propertied classes of the millions of peasants, and thus keep the whole people in darkness and subjection. The most outstanding among these relics of the past, the mightiest bulwark of all this barbarism, is the tsarist autocracy. By its very name it is bound to be hostile to any social movement, and cannot but be bitterly opposed to all the aspirations of the proletariat toward freedom.

To Establish a Democratic Republic

The Russian Social Democratic Labour Party therefore sets as its immediate political task the overthrow of the tsarist autocracy and its replacement by a democratic republic whose constitution would guarantee:

1. The sovereignty of the people; i.e., the concentration of the supreme power of the state in a unicameral legislative assembly composed of representatives of the people.

2. Universal, equal and direct suffrage for all citizens, male and female, who have reached the age of twenty; . . . a secret ballot in these elections. . . .

3. Broad local self-government; regional self-government for localities with special conditions of life or a particular make-up of the population.

4. Inviolability of person and dwelling.

5. Unrestricted freedom of conscience, speech, press and assembly; the right to strike and to form trade unions.

6. Freedom of movement and occupation.

7. Elimination of class privileges and the complete equality of all regardless of sex, religion, race or nationality.

8. The right of any person to obtain an education in their native language . . . ; the use of the native language together with the state language in all local, public and state institutions.

9. National self-determination for all nations forming part of the state.

10. The right of every person through normal channels to prosecute before a jury any official.

11. The popular election of judges.

12. The replacement of the standing army by the general arming of the population (i.e, the formation of a people's militia).

13. Separation of church and state, and of school and church.

14. Free and compulsory general or vocational education for all children of both sexes up to the age of sixteen; provision by the state of food, clothes, and school supplies for poor children.

As a fundamental condition for the democratisation of our national economy, the RSDRP demands the abolition of all indirect taxation and the introduction of a graduated tax on incomes and inheritances.

To Provide Protection for the Working Class

To protect the working class from physical and moral degradation, and also to develop its capacity for the liberation struggle; the party demands:

1. Limitation of the working day to eight hours for all hired workers. . . .

2. A complete ban on overtime work.

3. A ban on night work . . . with the exception of those (industries) which absolutely require it for technical reasons. . . .

4. The prohibition of the employment of children of school age. . . .

5. A ban on the use of female labour in occupations which are harmful to the health of women; maternity leave from four weeks prior to childbirth until six weeks after birth. . . .

6. The provision of nurseries for infants and young children in all . . . enterprises employing women.

7. State insurance for workers against old age and partial or complete disability through a special fund supported by a tax on capitalists. . . .

8. The appointment of an adequate number of factory inspectors in all branches of the economy. . . .

9. The supervision by organs of local self-government, together with elected workers' representatives, of sanitary conditions in factory housing. . . .

10. The establishment of properly organised health inspection in all enterprises . . . free medical services for workers at the employer's expense, with wages to be paid during time of illness.

11. Establishment of criminal responsibility of employers for violations of laws intended to protect workers.

12. The establishment in all branches of the economy of industrial tribunals made up equally of representatives of the workers and of management.

13. Imposition upon the organs of local self-government of the duty of establishing employment agencies (labour exchanges) to deal with the hiring of local and non-local labour in all branches of industry, and participation of workers' and employers' representatives in their administration.

To Eliminate the Remnants of Serfdom

In order to eliminate the remnants of serfdom, which lie as an oppressive burden on the peasantry, and to further the free development of the class struggle in the countryside, the party demands above all:

1. Abolition of redemption payments[1] and quit rents as well as all

1. payments for redemption loans, which were loans peasants were forced to take from the Russian government after the abolition of serfdom in 1861 in order to purchase land from noble landlords

obligations which presently fall on the peasantry, the tax-paying class.

2. The repeal of all laws hampering the peasant's disposal of his own land.

3. The return to the peasants of all moneys taken from them in the form of redemption payments and quit rents; the confiscation, for this purpose, of monastic and church property as well as of lands owned by the emperor, government agencies and members of the tsar's family; the imposition of a special tax on estates of the land-owning nobility who have availed themselves of the redemption loans; the deposit of sums obtained in this way into a special fund for the cultural and charitable needs of the village communities.

4. The institution of peasant committees:

  a. for the return to village communities (through expropriation or, if the lands have passed into other hands, through purchase by the state at the expense of the large holdings of the nobility) of lands cut off from peasant ownership at the time of the abolition of serfdom and which are now used by the landowners as a means of keeping the peasants in bondage;

  b. to transfer to peasant ownership those lands in the Caucasus which they use at the moment on a temporary basis;

  c. to eliminate the remnants of serfdom still in effect in the Urals, the Altai, the Western provinces, and other parts of the country.

5. The granting to the courts of the right to reduce excessively high rents and to declare null and void all transactions reflecting relations of servitude.

In striving to achieve its immediate goals, the RSDRP will support any opposition or revolutionary movement directed against the existing social and political order in Russia. At the same time, it resolutely rejects all reformist projects involving any broadening or strengthening of police or bureaucratic tutelage over the toiling classes.

The RSDRP, for its part, is firmly convinced that the complete, consistent and lasting realisation of these political and social changes can only be achieved through the overthrow of the autocracy and the convocation of a constituent assembly freely elected by the entire nation.

Viewpoint 3

"To call at present for an armed uprising means to stake on one card . . . the fate of the Russian and international revolution."

The Bolsheviks Should Not Seize Power

Lev Kamenev and Grigori Zinoviev

Lev Kamenev and Grigori Zinoviev were both leading members of the Russian Social Democratic Labor Party (the Bolsheviks). They played important roles in the Russian Revolution of 1917 and in the Soviet government after the revolution. In this document, written in October 1917, just prior to the revolution, Kamenev and Zinoviev oppose the idea of an immediate Bolshevik seizure of power. They argue that such an act would be premature as the conditions are not right for a Bolshevik victory. In particular, they contend that the majority of Russian people do not support the Bolsheviks and that the party is not yet strong enough to carry out a power play. Furthermore, they insist that the party should await the convening of the Constituent Assembly, which was promised by the Provisional Government holding power after the czar's abdication in March 1917. The Constituent Assembly was intended to be the representative body

Lev Kamenev and Grigori Zinoviev, letter to the Petrograd, Moscow, Moscow Regional, and Finnish Regional Committees of the R.S.D.L.P., the Bolshevik Group of the C.E.C. of the Soviets of Workers' and Soldiers' Deputies, and the Bolshevik Group of the Congress of the Soviets of the Northern Region, October 24, 1917.

elected by wide voter suffrage that would determine the course of Russia's future government. Kamenev and Zinoviev assert that by the time the Assembly is held (it was set for February 1918), the Bolsheviks will have achieved much more support and will be able to legally gain control of the government.

On the Present Situation

In labour circles there is developing and growing a current of thought which sees the only outcome in the immediate declaration of an armed uprising. The interaction of all the conditions at present is such that if we are to speak of such an uprising a definite date must be set for it, and that within the next few days. . . .

We are deeply convinced that to call at present for an armed uprising means to stake on one card not only the fate of our party, but also the fate of the Russian and international revolution.

There is no doubt that there are historical situations when an oppressed class must recognise that it is better to go forward to defeat than to give up without a battle. Does the Russian working class find itself at present in such a situation? *No*, and *a thousand times no!!!*

We Should Await the Convening of the Constituent Assembly

As a result of the immense growth of the influence of our party in the cities, and particularly in the army, there has come about at present a situation such that it is becoming more and more impossible for the bourgeoisie to obstruct the Constituent Assembly [the representative body to be elected and convened in February 1918 that was to determine the future course of Russia's government]. Through the army, through the workers, we hold a revolver at the temple of the bourgeoisie: the bourgeoisie is put in such a position that if it should undertake now to attempt to obstruct the Constituent Assembly, it would again push the petty-bourgeois parties to one side, and the revolver would go off.

The chances of our party in the elections to the Constituent Assembly are excellent. The talk that the influence of Bolshevism is beginning to wane, etc., we consider to have absolutely no foundation. In the mouths of our political opponents this assertion is simply a move in the political game, having as its purpose this very thing, to provoke an uprising of the Bolsheviks under conditions favourable to our enemies. The influence of the Bolsheviks is increasing. . . .

The Constituent Assembly, by itself, cannot of course abolish the present camouflaging of these interrelations. The Soviets, which have become rooted in life, can not be destroyed. The Constituent Assembly will be able to find support for its revolutionary work only in the Soviets. The Constituenf Assembly plus the Soviets—this is the combined type of state institutions toward which we are going. It is on this political basis that our party is acquiring enormous chances for a real victory.

We have never said that the Russian working class *alone*, by its own forces, would be able to bring the present revolution to a victorious conclusion. We have not forgotten, must not forget even now, that between us and the bourgeoisie there stands a huge third camp: the petty bourgeoisie. This camp joined us during the days of the Kornilov affair [the failed attempt by General Lavr Kornilov to seize power in August 1917] and gave us victory. It will join us many times more. We must not permit ourselves to be hypnotised by what is the case at the present moment. Undoubtedly, at present this camp is much nearer to the bourgeoisie than to us. But the present situation is not eternal, nor even durable. And only by a careless step, by some hasty action which will make the whole fate of the revolution dependent upon an immediate uprising, will the proletarian party push the petty bourgeoisie into the arms of [Minister of Public Affairs Pavel] Milyukov. . . .

The Majority Is *Not* with Us

We are told: (1) that the majority of the people of Russia is already with us, and (2) that the majority of the international proletariat is with us. Alas!—neither the one nor the other is true, and this is the crux of the entire situation. . . .

In what perspective then does the immediate future present itself to us? Here is our answer.

It stands to reason that our path does not depend upon ourselves alone. The enemy *may compel* us to accept decisive battle before the elections to the Constituent Assembly. Attempts at a new Kornilov affair will of course not leave us even the elections. We will then, of course, be unanimous, in the only possible decision. But at that time a substantial part of the petty-bourgeois camp too will surely support us again. The flight of the government to Moscow will push the masses of the petty bourgeoisie over to us. . . .

But in so far as the choice depends upon us, we can and we must limit ourselves to a *defensive position*. The Provisional Government is often powerless to carry into execution its counter-revolutionary intentions. . . . The strength of the soldiers and workers is sufficient to prevent the realisation of such steps by [Alexander] Kerensky [Prime Minister of the Provisional Government] and Company. The peasant movement has only just begun. The mass suppression of the peasant movement by the Cadets [Constitutional Democrats] cannot succeed with the sentiment of the army as it now is. The Provisional Government is powerless to fix up the elections to the Constituent Assembly. Sympathy with our party will grow. The bloc of the Cadets, the Mensheviks [rival Marxist party in Russia], and the S.-R.'s [Socialist Revolutionaries] will fall apart. In the Constituent Assembly we shall be such a strong opposition party that in a country of universal suffrage our opponents will be compelled to make concessions to us at every step, or we will form, together with the Left S.-R.'s, non-party peasants, etc., a ruling bloc which will fundamentally have to carry out our programme. This is our opinion.

An Armed Uprising Would Lead to Defeat

Before history, before the international proletariat, before the Russian Revolution and the Russian working class, we have no right to stake the whole future on the card of an armed uprising. It would be a mistake to think that such action now would, if it were unsuccessful, lead only to such consequences as did July 16–18 [Bolshevik demonstrations]. Now it is a question of something more. It is a question of decisive battle, and defeat in *that* battle would spell defeat to the revolution.

This is the general situation. But everyone who does not want merely to talk about uprising must carefully weigh its chances. And here we consider it our duty to say that at the present moment it would be most harmful to underestimate the forces of our opponent and overestimate our own forces. The forces of the opponent are greater than they appear. Petrograd is decisive, and in Petrograd the enemies of the proletarian party have accumulated substantial forces: 5,000 military cadets, *excellently* armed, *organised, anxious*, . . . and able to fight, also the staff, shock troops, Cossacks, a substantial part of the garrison, and very considerable artillery, which has taken up a position in fan-like formation around Petrograd. . . . The proletarian party at the present time would have to fight under an entirely different interrelationship of forces than in the days of the Kornilov affair. At that time we fought together with the S.-R.'s, the Mensheviks, and to some extent even with the adherents of Kerensky. Now, however, the proletarian party would have to fight against the Black Hundreds [gangs of anti-Semitic, anti-Socialist thugs] plus the Cadets, plus Kerensky and the Provisional Government, plus the S.-R.'s and Mensheviks.

The forces of the proletarian party are, of course, very substantial, but the decisive question is, is the sentiment among the workers and soldiers of the capital really such that they see salvation only in street fighting, that they are impatient to go into the streets? No. There is no such sentiment. Even those in favour of the uprising state that the sentiment of the masses of workers and soldiers is not at all even like their sentiments upon the eve of July 16. If among the great masses of the poor of the capital there were a militant sentiment burning to go into the streets, it might have served as a guarantee that an uprising initiated by them would draw in the biggest organisations (railroad unions, unions of postoffice and telegraph workers, etc.), where the influence of our party is weak. But since there is no such sentiment even in the factories and barracks, it would be self-deception to build any plans on it.

We are told: but the railroad workers and the postoffice and telegraph employees are starving, are crushed by poverty, are exasperated with the Provisional Government. All this is so, of course. But all this is still no guarantee that they will support an uprising against the government, in spite of the S.-R.'s and Mensheviks. The railroad workers and employees were crushed by poverty also in

1906, even as they are now in Germany and France. . . . If all these people who are crushed by poverty were always ready to support the armed uprising of the Socialists, we would have won Socialism long ago.

Consolidation Is Needed

This emphasises our immediate task. The Congress of Soviets has been called for November 2. It must be convened, no matter what the cost. It must organisationally consolidate the growing influence of the proletarian party. It must become the centre of the consolidation around the Soviets of all proletarian and semi-proletarian organisations, such as those same railroad unions, unions of postoffice and telegraph employees, bank employees, etc. As yet there is no firm organisational connection between these organisations and the Soviets. This cannot be considered as other than a symptom of the organisational weakness of the proletarian party. But such a connection is in any case a preliminary condition for the actual carrying out of the slogan, "All power to the Soviets." For any given moment this slogan naturally signifies the most decisive resistance to the slightest encroachment on the rights of the Soviets and organisations created by them, on the part of the government.

Under these conditions it would be a serious historical untruth to formulate the question of the transfer of power into the hands of the proletarian party in the terms: either now or never. . . . The party of the proletariat will grow. Its programme will become known to broader and broader masses. It will have the opportunity to continue on an even larger scale the merciless exposure of the policy of the Mensheviks and S.-R.'s who stand in the way of actual transfer of the power into the hands of the majority of the people. And there is only one way in which the proletarian party can interrupt its successes, and that is if under present conditions it take upon itself to initiate an uprising and thus expose the proletariat to the blows of the entire consolidated counter-revolution, supported by the petty-bourgeois democracy.

Against this perilous policy we raise our voice in warning.

Viewpoint 4

"To doubt now that the majority of the people are following and will follow the Bolsheviks is shameful vacillation and . . . is the abandoning of all *the principles of proletarian revolutionism."*

The Bolsheviks Should Seize Power

Vladimir I. Lenin

Vladimir I. Lenin was the founder of the Bolshevik Party (formed after a split with the Russian Social Democrats in 1903) and the most influential Russian Marxist. He had been forced to live abroad due to his revolutionary activities, but after the fall of the czarist government in 1917, he returned to Russia. Once back in Russia he and his associates began planning for the Socialist revolution they now believed to be inevitable. In this article Lenin counters those who oppose a Bolshevik seizure of power, arguing that the situation demands immediate action. He contests their assertions that the majority of Russian people do not support the Bolsheviks and that the Bolshevik Party is not strong enough to take power yet. Furthermore, he argues that waiting for the Constituent Assembly (the representative body that was to be held in February 1918) to convene does nothing to help the masses, who are facing starvation during an imminent famine. Lenin contends that the Provisional Government, a coalition of liberal democratic and Socialist parties

Vladimir I. Lenin, letter to Comrades, October 30, 1917.

formed after the fall of the czar in March, is not doing anything to aid the Russian people. Therefore, he asserts, the Bolsheviks must act. Lenin and his followers successfully carried out their plans and took control of the Russian government in November 1917. Lenin then went on to lead the newly created Soviet Union until his death in 1924.

Comrades,
We are living in a time that is so critical, events are moving at such incredible speed that a publicist, placed by the will of fate somewhat aside from the mainstream of history, constantly runs the risk either of being late or proving uninformed, especially if some time elapses before his writings appear in print. Although I fully realise this, I must nevertheless address this letter to the Bolsheviks, even at the risk of its not being published at all, for the vacillations against which I deem it my duty to warn in the most decisive manner are of an unprecedented nature and may have a disastrous effect on the Party, the movement of the international proletariat, and the revolution. As for the danger of being too late, I will prevent it by indicating the nature and date of the information I possess.

It was not until Monday morning, October 16, that I saw a comrade who had on the previous day participated in a very important Bolshevik gathering in Petrograd, and who informed me in detail of the discussion. The subject of discussion was that same question of the uprising discussed by the Sunday papers of all political trends. The gathering represented all that is most influential in all branches of Bolshevik work in the capital. Only a most insignificant minority of the gathering, namely, all in all two comrades, took a negative stand. The arguments which those comrades advanced are so weak, they are a manifestation of such an astounding confusion, timidity, and collapse of all the fundamental ideas of Bolshevism and proletarian revolutionary internationalism that it is not easy to discover an explanation for such shameful vacillations. The fact, however, remains, and since the revolutionary party has no right to tolerate vacillations on such a serious question, and since this pair of comrades, who have scattered their principles to the winds, might cause some confusion, it is necessary to analyse their arguments, to expose their vacillations, and to show how shameful they are. The following lines are an attempt to do this.

The Bolsheviks Do Have a Majority Among the People

"We have no majority among the people, and without this condition the uprising is hopeless...." People who can say this are either distorters of the truth or pedants who want an advance guarantee that throughout the whole country the Bolshevik Party has received exactly one-half of the votes plus one, this they want at all events, without taking the least account of the real circumstances of the revolution. History has never given such a guarantee, and is quite unable to give it in any revolution. To make such a demand is jeering at the audience, and is nothing but a cover to hide one's own *flight* from reality.

For reality shows us clearly that it was after the July days [Bolshevik-led demonstrations demanding food, land redistribution, and an end to World War I] that the majority of the people began quickly to go over to the side of the Bolsheviks. This was demonstrated first by the August 20 elections in Petrograd, ... when the Bolshevik vote rose from 20 to 33 per cent in the city not including the suburbs, and then by the district council elections in Moscow in September, when the Bolshevik vote rose from 11 to 49.3 per cent (one Moscow comrade, whom I saw recently, told me that the correct figure is 51 per cent). This was proved by the new elections to the Soviets [councils of workers, peasants, and soldiers that decided issues of local government]. It was proved by the fact that a majority of the peasant Soviets ... has expressed itself *against* the coalition. To be against the coalition means *in practice* to follow the Bolsheviks. Furthermore, reports from the front prove more frequently and more definitely that the soldiers are passing *en masse* over to the side of the Bolsheviks with ever greater determination, in spite of the malicious slanders and attacks by the Socialist-Revolutionary and Menshevik leaders, officers, deputies, etc., etc.

Last, but not least, the most outstanding fact of present day Russian life is *the revolt of the peasantry.* This shows objectively, not by words but by deeds, that the people are going over to the side of the Bolsheviks. . . . The peasant movement in Tambov Gubernia was an uprising both in the physical and political sense, an uprising that has yielded such splendid political results as, in the first place, agreement to transfer the land to the peasants. . . . This is a fact and facts are stubborn things. And such a factual "argument" *in favour* of an uprising is stronger than thousands of "pessimistic" evasions on the part of confused and frightened politicians. . . .

Another splendid political and revolutionary consequence of the peasant uprising, as already noted in [the Bolshevik newspaper] *Rabochy Put*, is the delivery of grain to the railway stations in Tambov Gubernia. Here is another "argument" for you, confused gentlemen, an argument in favour of the uprising as the only means to save the country from the famine that is knocking at our door and from a crisis of unheard-of dimensions. While the Socialist-Revolutionary and Menshevik betrayers of the people are grumbling, threatening, writing resolutions, promising to feed the hungry by convening the Constituent Assembly, the people are beginning to solve the bread problem *Bolshevik-fashion, by rebelling* against the landowners, capitalists, and speculators. . . .

To doubt now that the majority of the people are following and will follow the Bolsheviks is shameful vacillation and in practice is the abandoning of *all* the principles of proletarian revolutionism, the complete renunciation of Bolshevism.

The Bolsheviks Are Strong Enough to Take Power

"We are not strong enough to seize power, and the bourgeoisie is not strong enough to hinder the convening of the Constituent Assembly."

The first part of this argument is a simple paraphrase of the preceding one. It does not gain in strength or power of conviction, when the confusion of its authors and their fear of the bourgeoisie are expressed in terms of pessimism in respect of the workers and optimism in respect of the bourgeoisie. If the officer cadets and the Cossacks say that they will fight against the Bolsheviks to the last drop of blood, this deserves full credence; if, however, the workers and soldiers at hundreds of meetings express full confidence in the Bolsheviks and affirm their readiness to defend the transfer of power to the Soviets, then it is "timely" to recall that voting is one thing and fighting another!

If you argue like that, of course, you "refute" the possibility of an uprising. But, we may ask, in what way does this peculiarly orientated "pessimism" with its peculiar urge differ from a political shift to the side of the bourgeoisie?

Look at the facts. Remember the Bolshevik declarations, repeated thousands of times and now "forgotten" by our pessimists. We have said thousands of times that the Soviets of Workers' and Soldiers' Deputies are a force, that they are the vanguard of the revolution, that they *can* take power....

The Revolution Cannot Wait Any Longer

"We are becoming stronger every day. We can enter the Constituent Assembly as a strong opposition; why should we stake everything? ... "

This is the argument of a philistine who has "read" that the Constituent Assembly is being called, and who trustingly acquiesces in the most legal, most loyal, most constitutional course. It is a pity, however, that *waiting* for the Constituent Assembly does not solve either the question of famine or the question of surrendering Petrograd. This "trifle" is forgotten by the naïve or the confused or those who have allowed themselves to be frightened.

The famine will not wait. The peasant uprising did not wait. The war will not wait. The admirals who have disappeared did not wait.

Will the famine agree to wait, because we Bolsheviks *proclaim* faith in the convocation of the Constituent Assembly?

CHAPTER 2

What Foreign Policy Should the Soviets Pursue?

 Chapter Preface

From its very inception, the Soviet Union experienced numerous difficulties in its relations with the rest of the world. Following the revolution of 1917, many countries refused to recognize the legitimacy of the new Bolshevik government. Some, including the United States and Great Britain, even voiced their objection to Soviet rule by sending their troops to fight the Bolsheviks in the Russian Civil War of 1918–1921. The Soviet Union's subsequent foreign policy was largely shaped by the "siege mentality" that developed during the civil war. As a result, its relations with the rest of the world were often strained and tense. Yet the Soviets eventually realized that despite ideological differences they needed to participate in international diplomacy. Thus Soviet foreign policy often alternated between confrontation and cooperation and was shaped less by ideological considerations than by the need to maximize advantages in particular circumstances.

The apex of the USSR's efforts at international cooperation came when the Soviets joined the British, French, and, later, the Americans, in fighting the Germans and the Japanese during World War II. The alliance among these powers was forged mostly out of necessity rather than a true spirit of friendship. After the war the tenuous ties that held the Allies together began to slip away. The Red Army had liberated most of Eastern Europe from German control, and the Soviets believed they were entitled to control of these lands as a result of the tremendous sacrifices they had endured during the war, including a death toll well above 10 million. The two sides begrudgingly conceded "spheres of influence" to each other, with the USSR controlling most of Eastern Europe. But the tensions between the West and the Soviet Union escalated into a cold war. Each side vied for influence and control in Europe and around the world, particularly in developing countries, offering aid and assistance to various nations in Asia, Africa, and Latin America.

The Cold War between the Soviet Union and the West continued for forty-five years, until the demise of the USSR in 1991, and was accompanied by a massive arms buildup by both sides. During that period there were hot spots—flare-ups of tensions that sometimes led to military confrontations between the West and Communist regimes (as in the cases of Korea and Vietnam). Only once, however, during the Cuban missile crisis of 1962, did the two superpowers (the United States and the Soviet Union) come very close to actually fighting each other directly. Nevertheless, as historian Nicholas Riasanovsky states, the Soviet Union continued to try to extend its power in the world by "pushing hard Soviet influence and interests in Europe, Asia, the Near East, Africa and elsewhere."

Despite this atmosphere of tension and suspicion, cooperation did occur between the West and the Soviet Union, particularly after the death of Joseph Stalin. There were long periods of peaceful coexistence and détente, when the two sides lived in relative toleration of one another, despite cutting rhetoric. The risk of mutually assured destruction as a result of the vast arsenals of nuclear weapons held by each country, in theory, deterred direct military confrontation and in fact fostered the need for cooperation. The USSR collaborated extensively with the United States in an effort to control and reduce nuclear arms and testing, both in their own countries and among other nuclear powers. In the end, while the Soviets maintained a guarded stance in their foreign policy, they also opened their country to new influences and the possibility of participation in the global community.

Viewpoint 1

"Only the victory of the proletariat in the West could protect Russia from bourgeois restoration."

The Revolution Must Be Spread to the West to Ensure the Success of Russian Socialism

Leon Trotsky

One of the main tenets of Karl Marx's Socialist theory was that the Socialist revolution must be spread throughout the world in order to succeed. Despite the success of the Russian Marxists in their revolution in 1917, other countries failed to follow suit. In fact, many Western nations reacted to the Communist victory with fear and apprehension, and some even sent troops to fight the Bolsheviks during the Russian Civil War (1918–1921). Therefore, a number of Bolsheviks began to think that they would have to continue their struggle alone, without a world-wide revolution. In the mid-1920s the issue became a serious point of contention among leading Bolsheviks, and factions formed around the opposing views. Leon Trotsky emerged as the leading proponent of the theory of "permanent revolution," the term used to describe revolutionary ferment spreading from

Leon Trotsky, *Stalin, an Appraisal of the Man and His Influence.* New York: Harper & Brothers, 1941.

one country to another. In this article Trotsky outlines his view that without a worldwide revolution, socialism would never succeed in Russia. Thus, he argues, the Bolsheviks were obligated to support revolutionary movements in other nations, while simultaneously supporting a militant Socialist policy at home.

Trotsky was one of the most important members of the early Bolshevik party. He was responsible for organizing the military activities of the Communists during the revolution and the ensuing civil war. Many believed he would succeed Vladimir I. Lenin as leader of the Communist Party and thus the Soviet government, but he was ousted by Joseph Stalin and eventually exiled from Russia. He fled to Mexico in the 1940s, where he was murdered, presumably on Stalin's orders.

Russia's development is first of all notable for its backwardness. But historical backwardness does not mean a mere retracing of the course of the advanced countries a hundred or two hundred years late. Rather, it gives rise to an utterly different "combined" social formation, in which the most highly developed achievements of capitalist technique and structure are integrated into the social relations of feudal and pre-feudal barbarism, transforming and dominating them, fashioning a unique relationship of classes. The same is true of ideas. Precisely because of its historical tardiness, Russia proved to be the only European country in which Marxism, as a doctrine, and the Social Democracy, as a party, enjoyed a powerful development even prior to the bourgeois revolution—and naturally so, because the problem of the relation between the struggle for democracy and the struggle for socialism was subjected to the most profound theoretical examination in Russia....

The Theory of Permanent Revolution

After writing my pamphlet, "Until the Ninth of January," I repeatedly returned to the development and the grounding of the theory of permanent revolution. In view of the significance it subsequently acquired in the intellectual evolution of the hero of this biography [Joseph Stalin], it is necessary to present it here in the form of exact quotations from my works of the years 1905 and 1906.

The nucleus of population in a contemporary city—at least, in a city of economic and political significance—is the sharply differentiated class of hired labor. It is this class, essentially unknown to the Great French Revolution, which is fated to play the decisive role in our revolution. . . . In an economically more backward country the proletariat may come to power sooner than in a country more advanced capitalistically. The conception of a kind of automatic dependence of the proletarian dictatorship on a country's technical forces and means is a prejudice of extremely simplified "economic" materialism. Such a view has nothing in common with Marxism. . . . Notwithstanding the fact that the productive forces of United States industry are ten times greater than ours, the political role of the Russian proletariat, its influence on the politics of its own country and the possibility that it may soon influence world politics are incomparably greater than the role of significance of the American proletariat. . . .

It seems to me that the Russian Revolution will create such conditions that the power may (in the event of victory, *must*) pass into the hands of the proletariat before the politicians of bourgeois liberalism will find it possible fully to unfold their genius for statecraft. . . . The Russian bourgeoisie will surrender all the revolutionary positions to the proletariat. It will also have to surrender revolutionary hegemony over the peasantry. The proletariat in power will come to the peasantry as the class liberator. . . . The proletariat, leaning on the peasantry, will bring into motion all the forces for raising the cultural level of the village and for developing political consciousness in the peasantry. . . .

But will not perhaps the peasantry itself drive the proletariat away and supersede it? That is impossible. All historic experience repudiates that supposition. It shows that the peasantry is utterly incapable of an *independent* political role. . . . From the aforesaid it is clear how I look upon the idea of the "dictatorship of the proletariat and the peasantry." The point is not whether I deem it admissible in principle, whether I "want" or "do not want" such a form of political cooperation. I deem it unrealizable—at least, in the direct and immediate sense.

The foregoing already shows how incorrect is the assertion that the conception here expounded "jumped over the bourgeois revolution," as has been subsequently reiterated without end. "The struggle for the democratic renovation of Russia . . ." I wrote at the same time, "is in its entirety derived from capitalism, is being conducted by forces formed on the basis of capitalism, and *immediately, in the first place*, is directed against the feudal and vassal obstacles that stand in the way of developing a capitalist society." But the substance of the question was with what forces and by which methods these obstacles could be overcome. . . .

The Success of Revolution in Russia Is Dependent on Europe

> But we may already ask ourselves: must the dictatorship of the proletariat[1] inevitably smash itself against the framework of the bourgeois revolution or can it, on the basis of the existing historical situation of the *world*, look forward to the perspective of victory, after smashing this limiting framework? . . . One thing may be said with certainty: without the direct governmental support of the European proletariat, the working class of Russia will not be able to maintain itself in power and transform its temporary reign into an enduring socialist dictatorship.

But this does not necessarily lead to a pessimistic prognosis:

> The political liberation, led by the working class of Russia, will raise the leader to a height unprecedented in history, transmit to him colossal forces and means, and make him the initiator of the world-wide liquidation of capitalism, for which history has created all the objective prerequisites.

As to the extent to which international Social Democracy will prove capable of fulfilling its revolutionary task, I wrote in 1906:

> The European socialist parties—and in the first place, the mightiest of them, the German party—have developed their

---

1. According to Marxist theory, the dictatorship of the proletariat is a stage in the transition from capitalism to communism. During this phase, the working class uses state power to quell opposition and control the means of production.

conservatism, which grows stronger in proportion to the size of the masses embraced by socialism and the effectiveness of the organization and the discipline of these masses. Because of that, the Social Democracy, as the organization that embodies the political experience of the proletariat, may at a given moment become the immediate obstacle on the path of an open clash between the workers and the bourgeois reaction.

Yet I concluded my analysis by expressing the assurance that

the Eastern revolution will infect the Western proletariat with revolutionary idealism and arouse in it the desire to start talking "Russian" with its enemy. . . .

The Only Sure Path to Socialism

The perspective of permanent revolution may be summarized in the following way: the complete victory of the democratic revolution in Russia is conceivable only in the form of the dictatorship of the proletariat, leaning on the peasantry. The dictatorship of the proletariat, which would inevitably place on the order of the day not only democratic but socialistic tasks as well, would at the same time give a powerful impetus to the international socialist revolution. Only the victory of the proletariat in the West could protect Russia from bourgeois restoration and assure it the possibility of rounding out the establishment of socialism.

That compact formula discloses with equal distinctness the similarity of the latter two concepts in their irreconcilable differentiation from the liberal Menshevik perspective as well as their extremely essential distinction from each other on the question of the social character and the tasks of the "dictatorship" which must grow out of the revolution. The not infrequent complaint in the writings of the present Moscow theoreticians that the program of the dictatorship of the proletariat was "premature" in 1905 is beside the point. In an empirical sense the program of the democratic dictatorship of the proletariat and the peasantry proved equally "premature." The unfavorable combination of forces at the time of the First Revolution [in 1905] did not so much preclude the dictatorship of the proletariat as the victory of the revolution in general. Yet all the revolutionary groups were based on the hope of complete victory; the supreme revolutionary struggle would have been impossible without such a hope. The differences of opinion dealt with the general perspective of the revolution and the strategy arising from that. The perspective of Menshevism was false to the core: it pointed out the wrong road to the proletariat. The perspective of Bolshevism was not complete: it correctly pointed out the general direction of the struggle, but characterized its stages incorrectly. The insufficiency in the perspective of Bolshevism did not become apparent in 1905 only because the revolution itself did not undergo further development. But then at the beginning of 1917 Lenin was obliged to alter his perspective, in direct conflict with the old cadres of his party.

No political prognosis can pretend to be mathematically exact; suffice it if it correctly indicates the general line of development and helps to orient the actual course of events, which inevitably bends the main line right and left. In that sense it is impossible not to see that the concept of permanent revolution has completely passed the test of history. During the initial years of the Soviet regime no one denied that; on the contrary, that fact found acknowledgment in a number of official publications. But when the bureaucratic reaction against October opened up in the calmed and cooled upper crust of Soviet society, it was at once directed against the theory which reflected the first proletarian revolution more completely than anything else while at the same time openly exposing its unfinished, limited, and partial character. Thus, by way of repulsion, originated the theory of socialism in a separate country, the basic dogma of Stalinism.

Viewpoint 2

"According to [Vladimir I.] Lenin, the revolution draws its strength primarily from among the workers and peasants of Russia."

Socialism Can Succeed in Russia Without Being Spread Abroad

Joseph Stalin

The debate over whether socialism could succeed in Russia without an international revolution intensified in the mid-1920s and became one of the focal points of the struggle for power that ensued after Lenin's death in 1924. Joseph Stalin was a leading Bolshevik and commissar of Nationalities in the new Soviet state during this time. He was determined to become Lenin's successor and would use any means necessary to discredit and defeat his opponents in order to achieve this goal. Trotsky was his main opponent in the struggle for power. Therefore, he denounced Trotsky's theory of permanent revolution and insisted that it was necessary to construct and consolidate the already existing Socialist system in Russia before attempting to ignite revolutions abroad. In this article he argues his theory of "socialism in one

Joseph Stalin, "The October Revolution and the Tactics of the Russian Communists," www.marx2mao.com.

country," which he asserts is more consistent with the tenets put forth by Vladimir I. Lenin on the nature of the revolution. He accuses Trotsky of betraying the ideas of Lenin and of lacking confidence in the Russian people to build a Socialist state. He rejects Trotsky's notion that Russian socialism needs the support of the European workers and instead asserts that Russian socialism can serve as the model for revolutions in other countries. The rest of the party found Stalin's theory of "socialism in one country" more appealing than Trotsky's concept of "permanent revolution." Many saw support of revolutions abroad to be too risky and too expensive for the new, struggling Soviet state. They were more concerned about getting the war-torn and economically devastated country back on its feet.

According to [Vladimir I.] Lenin, the revolution draws its strength primarily from among the workers and peasants of Russia itself. According to [Leon] Trotsky, the necessary strength can be found *only* "in the arena of the world proletarian revolution."

But what if the world revolution is fated to arrive with some delay? Is there any ray of hope for our revolution? Trotsky offers no ray of hope, for "the contradictions in the position of a workers' government . . . can be solved *only* . . . in the arena of the world proletarian revolution." According to this plan, there is but one prospect left for our revolution: to vegetate in its own contradictions and rot away while waiting for the world revolution. . . .

"Permanent revolution" is not a mere underestimation of the revolutionary potentialities of the peasant movement. "Permanent revolution" is an underestimation of the peasant movement which leads to the *repudiation* of Lenin's theory of the dictatorship of the proletariat [the stage of communism wherein the working class controls the government].

Trotsky's "permanent revolution" is a variety of *Menshevism* [the Mensheviks were another Marxist party]. . . .

Lenin's Views

The second peculiar feature of the October Revolution lies in the fact that this revolution represents a model of the practical application of Lenin's theory of the proletarian revolution.

He who has not understood this peculiar feature of the October Revolution will never understand either the international nature of this revolution, or its colossal international might, or the specific features of its foreign policy. [According to Lenin,]

> Uneven economic and political development is an absolute law of capitalism. Hence, the victory of socialism is possible first in several or even in one separate capitalist country. The victorious proletariat of that country, having expropriated the capitalists and organized socialist production, would stand up *against* the rest of the world, the capitalist world, attracting to its cause the oppressed classes of other countries, raising revolts in those countries against the capitalists, and in the event of necessity coming out even with armed force against the exploiting classes and their states. For the free union of nations in socialism is impossible without a more or less prolonged and stubborn struggle of the socialist republics against the backward states.

The opportunists of all countries assert that the proletarian revolution can begin—if it is to begin anywhere at all, according to their theory—only in industrially developed countries, and that the more highly developed these countries are industrially the more chances there are for the victory of socialism. Moreover, according to them, the possibility of the victory of socialism in one country, and in a country little developed in the capitalist sense at that, is excluded as something absolutely improbable. As far back as the period of the war, Lenin, taking as his basis the law of the uneven development of the imperialist states, opposed to the opportunists his theory of the proletarian revolution on the victory of socialism in one country, even if that country is less developed in the capitalist sense.

It is well known that the October Revolution fully confirmed the correctness of Lenin's theory of the proletarian revolution.

Trotsky's Views

How do matters stand with Trotsky's "permanent revolution" in the light of Lenin's theory of the victory of the proletarian revolution in one country?

Let us take Trotsky's pamphlet *Our Revolution* (1906). Trotsky writes:

> Without direct state support from the European proletariat, the working class of Russia will not be able to maintain itself in power and to transform its temporary rule into a lasting socialist dictatorship. This we cannot doubt for an instant.

What does this quotation mean? It means that the victory of socialism in one country, in this case Russia, is impossible "*without* direct state support from the European proletariat," i.e., before the European proletariat has conquered power.

What is there in common between this "theory" and Lenin's thesis on the possibility of the victory of socialism "in one separate capitalist country"?

Clearly, there is nothing in common. . . .

It goes without saying that for the *complete* victory of socialism, for *complete* security against the restoration of the old order, the united efforts of the proletarians of several countries are necessary. It goes without saying that, without the support given to our revolution by the proletariat of Europe, the proletariat of Russia could not have held out against the general onslaught, just as without the support the revolution in Russia gave to the revolutionary movement in the West the latter could not have developed at the pace at which it has begun to develop since the establishment of the proletarian dictatorship in Russia. It goes without saying that we need support. But what does support of our revolution by the West-European proletariat imply? Is not the sympathy of European workers for our revolution, their readiness to thwart the imperialists' plans of intervention—is not all this support? Is this not real assistance? Unquestionably it is. . . .

Trotsky Does Not Believe in the Strength of Russian Socialism

Let us take, for example, Trotsky's "postscript," written in 1922, for the new edition of his pamphlet *Peace Program*. Here is what he says in this "Postscript":

> The assertion reiterated several times in the *Peace Program* that a proletarian revolution cannot culminate victoriously

within national bounds may perhaps seem to some readers to have been refuted by the nearly five years' experience of our Soviet republic. But such a conclusion would be unwarranted. The fact that the workers' state has held out against the whole world in one country, and a backward country at that, only testifies to the colossal might of the proletariat, which in other, more advanced, more civilized countries will be truly capable of performing miracles. But while we have held our ground as a state politically and militarily, we have not arrived, or even begun to arrive, at the building of a socialist society. . . . As long as the bourgeoisie remains in power in the other European countries we will be compelled, in our struggle against economic isolation, to strive for agreement with the capitalist world, at the same time it may be said with certainty that these agreements may at best help us to mitigate some of our economic ills, to take one or another step forward, but real progress of a socialist economy in Russia will become possible *only after the victory* of the proletariat in the major European countries. (Stalin's italics.)

Joseph Stalin

Thus speaks Trotsky, plainly sinning against reality and stubbornly trying to save his "permanent revolution" from final shipwreck.

It appears, then, that, twist and turn as you like, we not only have "not arrived," but we have "not even begun to arrive" at the building of a socialist society. It appears that some people have been hoping for "agreements with the capitalist world," but it also appears that nothing will come of these agreements, for, twist and turn as you like, a "real progress of a socialist economy" will not be possible until the proletariat has been victorious in the "major European countries."

Well, then, since there is still no victory in the West, the only "choice" that remains for the revolution in Russia is: either to rot away or to degenerate into a bourgeois state.

It is no accident that Trotsky has been talking for two years now about the "degeneration" of our Party. . . .

Trotsky's "permanent revolution" is the negation of Lenin's theory of the proletarian revolution; and conversely, Lenin's theory of the proletarian revolution is the negation of the theory of "permanent revolution."

Lack of faith in the strength and capabilities of our revolution, lack of faith in the strength and capabilities of the Russian proletariat—that is what lies at the root of the theory of "permanent revolution."

Hitherto only *one* aspect of the theory of "permanent revolution" has usually been noted—lack of faith in the revolutionary potentialities of the peasant movement. Now, in fairness, this must be supplemented by *another* aspect—lack of faith in the strength and capabilities of the proletariat in Russia.

What difference is there between Trotsky's theory and the ordinary Menshevik theory that the victory of socialism in one country, and in a backward country at that, is impossible without the preliminary victory of the proletarian revolution "in the principal countries of Western Europe"?

As a matter of fact, there is no difference.

There can be no doubt at all. Trotsky's theory of "permanent revolution" is a variety of Menshevism.

Viewpoint 3

"The foreign policy of the United States, which reflects the imperialist tendencies of American monopolistic capital, is characterized . . . by a striving for world supremacy."

The West Is a Dangerous Threat to the Soviet Union

Nikolai Novikov

Following the end of World War II, relations between the Soviet Union and the West became increasingly tense and confrontational. Despite the fact that they had been allies during the war, each side began to view the other with distrust. The Soviets intensified efforts to reduce Western influence and foster suspicion of the West. They portrayed the Western countries as enemies of communism whose goal was to destroy the Soviet system. In the United States and Great Britain, the Soviets were vilified as repressive and undemocratic. In 1946 an American diplomat in Moscow, George Kennan, composed a report characterizing the Soviets as unable to compromise with their rivals and bent on world domination. Shortly thereafter, Soviet chargé d'affaires in Washington, Nikolai Novikov, wrote a similar report, one that in many ways mirrored Kennan's. Novikov was highly concerned

Nikolai Novikov, "The Novikov Report," September 27, 1946.

about America's efforts to extend its influence in the world. He portrayed American interests as based on the drive to control the world, particularly its valuable resources, such as oil. The United States' policy toward the USSR, Novikov argued, was aimed at limiting or eliminating Soviet influence and stopping the processes of democratization. The Americans were using the threat of war to exert political pressure on the Soviet Union and force it to make concessions. In fact, Novikov maintained, the United States was preparing its military for just such a war, making it a dangerous foe. This was the beginning of the Cold War between the Soviet Union and the West, which was to last for forty-five years, until the collapse of the Soviet Union in 1991.

The foreign policy of the United States, which reflects the imperialist tendencies of American monopolistic capital, is characterized in the postwar period by a striving for world supremacy. This is the real meaning of the many statements by President Truman and other representatives of American ruling circles: that the United States has the right to lead the world. All the forces of American diplomacy—the army, the air force, the navy, industry, and science—are enlisted in the service of this foreign policy. For this purpose broad plans for expansion have been developed and are being implemented through diplomacy and the establishment of a system of naval and air bases stretching far beyond the boundaries of the United States, through the arms race, and through the creation of ever newer types of weapons.

U.S. Foreign Policy in the Postwar Period

1. a) The foreign policy of the United States is conducted now in a situation that differs greatly from the one that existed in the prewar period. . . .

b) . . . Europe has come out of the war with a completely dislocated economy, and the economic devastation that occurred in the course of the war cannot be overcome in a short time. All of the countries of Europe and Asia are experiencing a colossal need for consumer goods, industrial and transportation equipment, etc. Such a situation provides American monopolistic capital with prospects for enormous shipments of goods and the importation of capital into these countries—a circumstance that would permit it to infiltrate their national economies. . . .

c) . . . [W]e have [also] seen a failure of calculations on the part of U. S. circles which assumed that the Soviet Union would be destroyed in the war or would come out of it so weakened that it would be forced to go begging to the United States for economic assistance. Had that happened, they would have been able to dictate conditions permitting the United States to carry out its expansion in Europe and Asia without hindrance from the USSR.

In actuality, despite all of the economic difficulties of the postwar period connected with the enormous losses inflicted by the war and the German fascist occupation, the Soviet Union continues to remain economically independent of the outside world and is rebuilding its national economy with its own forces.

At the same time the USSR's international position is currently stronger than it was in the prewar period. Thanks to the historical victories of Soviet weapons, the Soviet armed forces are located on the territory of Germany and other formerly hostile countries, thus guaranteeing that these countries will not be used again for an attack on the USSR. . . .

Such a situation in Eastern and Southeastern Europe cannot help but be regarded by the American imperialists as an obstacle in the path of the expansionist policy of the United States.

U.S. Political Situation

2. a) The foreign policy of the United States is not determined at present by the circles in the Democratic party that (as was the case during Roosevelt's lifetime) strive to strengthen the cooperation of the three great powers that constituted the basis of the anti-Hitler coalition during the war. The ascendance to power of President Truman, a politically unstable person but with certain conservative tendencies, and the subsequent appointment of [James] Byrnes as Secretary of State meant a strengthening of the influence on U.S. foreign policy of the most reactionary circles of the Democratic party. . . .

b) At the same time, there has been a decline in the influence on foreign policy of those who follow Roosevelt's course for cooperation among peace-loving countries. Such persons in the government, in Congress, and in the leadership of the Democratic party are being pushed farther and farther into the background. The contradictions in the field of foreign policy existing between the followers of [Henry] Wallace and [Claude] Pepper, on the one hand, and the adherents of the reactionary "bi-partisan" policy, on the other, were manifested with great clarity recently in the speech by Wallace that led to his resignation from the post of Secretary of Commerce. . . .

3. Obvious indications of the U.S. effort to establish world dominance are also to be found in the increase in military potential in peacetime and in the establishment of a large number of naval and air bases both in the United States and beyond its borders.

In the summer of 1946, for the first time in the history of the country, Congress passed a law on the establishment of a peacetime army, not on a volunteer basis but on the basis of universal military service. The size of the army, which is supposed to amount to about one million persons as of July 1, 1947, was also increased significantly. The size of the navy at the conclusion of the war decreased quite insignificantly in comparison with wartime. At the present time, the American navy occupies first place in the world, leaving England's navy far behind, to say nothing of those of other countries. . . .

The establishment of American bases on islands that are often 10,000 to 12,000 kilometers from the territory of the United States and are on the other side of the Atlantic and Pacific oceans clearly indicates the offensive nature of the strategic concepts of the commands of the U.S. army and navy. . . .

All of these facts show clearly that a decisive role in the realization of plans for world dominance by the United States is played by its armed forces.

United States and England Aim at World Domination

4. a) One of the stages in the achievement of dominance over the world by the United States is its understanding with England concerning the partial division of the world on the basis of mutual concessions. The basic lines of the secret agreement between the

United States and England regarding the division of the world consist, as shown by facts, in their agreement on the inclusion of Japan and China in the sphere of influence of the United States in the Far East, while the United States, for its part, has agreed not to hinder England either in resolving the Indian problem or in strengthening its influence in Siam and Indonesia....

5. a) If the division of the world in the Far East between the United States and England may be considered an accomplished fact, it cannot be said that an analogous situation exists in the basin of the Mediterranean Sea and in the countries adjacent to it.... The United States ... is not interested in providing assistance and support to the British Empire in this vulnerable point, but rather in its own more thorough penetration of the Mediterranean basin and Near East, to which the United States is attracted by the area's natural resources, primarily oil....

c) The irregular nature of relations between England and the United States in the Near East is manifested in part also in the great activity of the American naval fleet in the eastern part of the Mediterranean Sea. Such activity cannot help but be in conflict with the basic interests of the British Empire....

It must be kept in mind, however, that [recent] incidents ... and the great interest that U.S. diplomacy displays in the problem of the [Turkish] straits have a double meaning. On the one hand, they indicate that the United States has decided to consolidate its position in the Mediterranean basin.... On the other hand, these incidents constitute a political and military demonstration against the Soviet Union. The strengthening of U.S. positions in the Near East ... will therefore signify the emergence of a new threat to the security of the southern regions of the Soviet Union....

U.S. Policy Toward the USSR

7. a) The "hard-line" policy with regard to the USSR announced by Byrnes after the rapprochement of the reactionary Democrats with the Republicans is at present the main obstacle on the road to cooperation of the Great Powers. It consists mainly of the fact that in the postwar period the United States no longer follows a policy of strengthening cooperation among the Big Three [the United States, France, and Britain] (or Four) [the Big Three plus

the Soviet Union] but rather has striven to undermine the unity of these countries. The objective has been to impose the will of other countries on the Soviet Union. . . .

b) The present policy of the American government with regard to the USSR is also directed at limiting or dislodging the influence of the Soviet Union from neighboring countries. In implementing this policy in former enemy or Allied countries adjacent to the USSR, the United States attempts, at various international conferences or directly in these countries themselves, to support reactionary forces with the purpose of creating obstacles to the process of democratization of these countries. In so doing, it also attempts to secure positions for the penetration of American capital into their economies. Such a policy is intended to weaken and overthrow the democratic governments in power there, which are friendly toward the USSR, and replace them in the future with new governments that would obediently carry out a policy dictated from the United States. In this policy, the United States receives full support from English diplomacy.

c) One of the most important elements in the general policy of the United States, which is directed toward limiting the international role of the USSR in the postwar world, is the policy with regard to Germany. In Germany, the United States is taking measures to strengthen reactionary forces for the purpose of opposing democratic reconstruction. Furthermore, it displays special insistence on accompanying this policy with completely inadequate measures for the demilitarization of Germany.

The American occupation policy does not have the objective of eliminating the remnants of German Fascism and rebuilding German political life on a democratic basis, so that Germany might cease to exist as an aggressive force. . . . Instead, the United States is considering the possibility of terminating the Allied occupation of German territory before the main tasks of the occupation—the demilitarization and democratization of Germany—have been implemented. This would create the prerequisites for the revival of an imperialistic Germany, which the United States plans to use in a future war on its side. One cannot help seeing that such a policy has a clearly outlined anti-Soviet edge and constitutes a serious danger to the cause of peace.

Hostile Statements

d) The numerous and extremely hostile statements by American government, political, and military figures with regard to the Soviet Union and its foreign policy are very characteristic of the current relationship between the ruling circles of the United States and the USSR. These statements are echoed in an even more unrestrained tone by the overwhelming majority of the American press organs. Talk about a "third war," meaning a war against the Soviet Union, and even a direct call for this war—with the threat of using the atomic bomb—such is the content of the statements on relations with the Soviet Union by reactionaries at public meetings and in the press. At the present time, preaching war against the Soviet Union is not a monopoly of the far-right, yellow American press represented by the newspaper associations of Hearst and McCormick. This anti-Soviet campaign also has been joined by the "reputable" and "respectable" organs of the conservative press, such as the *New York Times* and *New York Herald Tribune*....

The basic goal of this anti-Soviet campaign of American "public opinion" is to exert political pressure on the Soviet Union and compel it to make concessions. Another, no less important goal of the campaign is the attempt to create an atmosphere of war psychosis among the masses, who are weary of war, thus making it easier for the U.S. government to carry out measures for the maintenance of high military potential. It was in this very atmosphere that the law on universal military service in peacetime was passed by Congress, that the huge military budget was adopted, and that plans are being worked out for the construction of an extensive system of naval and air bases.

e) Of course, all of these measures for maintaining a high military potential are not goals in themselves. They are only intended to prepare the conditions for winning world supremacy in a new war, the date for which, to be sure, cannot be determined now by anyone, but which is contemplated by the most bellicose circles of American imperialism.

Careful note should be taken of the fact that the preparation by the United States for a future war is being conducted with the prospect of war against the Soviet Union, which in the eyes of American imperialists is the main obstacle in the path of the United

States to world domination. This is indicated by facts such as the tactical training of the American army for war with the Soviet Union as the future opponent, the siting of American strategic bases in regions from which it is possible to launch strikes on Soviet territory, intensified training and strengthening of Arctic regions as close approaches to the USSR, and attempts to prepare Germany and Japan to use those countries in a war against the USSR.

Viewpoint 4

"Nobody knows what Soviet Russia and its Communist international organization intends to do in the immediate future, or what are the limits, if any, to their expansive and proselytizing tendencies."

The Soviet Union and Communism Are Dangerous Threats to the West

Winston Churchill

Winston Churchill, prime minister of Great Britain during the Second World War, delivered this speech, which came to be known as the "iron curtain" speech, to an American audience in Fulton, Missouri, on March 5, 1946. The speech had a tremendous impact on the development of the Cold War between the Soviet Union and the West. In it, Churchill claims that the Soviets, by occupying lands or installing Communist governments in the countries of Eastern Europe, had dropped an "iron curtain" across the continent, behind which people lived under the repressive control of Moscow. He argues that the Soviet Union's

Winston Churchill, address at Fulton Missouri, March 5, 1946.

expansionist and totalitarian policies threatened the democracies of the world as well as the recently achieved world peace. He urges the United States and Great Britain to remain vigilant against this threat and not to appease the Soviet Union. Therefore, he concludes, it was necessary to maintain an armed force that was ready to combat Soviet aggression if the need arose.

Although Churchill was no longer the leader of the United Kingdom, he was still a highly revered and immensely popular figure. His words reflected the common feeling of both the American and British governments.

The United States stands at this time at the pinnacle of world power. It is a solemn moment for the American democracy. With primacy in power is also joined an awe-inspiring accountability to the future. As you look around you, you feel not only the sense of duty done but also feel anxiety lest you fall below the level of achievement. Opportunity is here now, clear and shining, for both our countries. To reject it or ignore it or fritter it away will bring upon us all the long reproaches of the after-time. It is necessary that constancy of mind, persistency of purpose, and the grand simplicity of decision shall guide and rule the conduct of the English-speaking peoples in peace as they did in war. We must and I believe we shall prove ourselves equal to this severe requirement. . . .

Before we cast away the solid assurances of national armaments for self-preservation, we must be certain that our temple is built, not upon shifting sands or quagmires, but upon the rock. Anyone with his eyes open can see that our path will be difficult and also long, but if we persevere together as we did in the two World Wars—though not, alas, in the interval between them—I cannot doubt that we shall achieve our common purpose in the end.

I have, however, a definite and practical proposal to make for action. Courts and magistrates cannot function without sheriffs and constables. The United Nations Organization must immediately begin to be equipped with an international armed force. In such a matter we can only go step by step; but we must begin now. I propose that each of the powers and states should be invited to dedicate a certain number of air squadrons to the service of the world organization. These squadrons would be trained and pre-pared in their own countries but would move around in rotation from one country to another. They would wear the uniform of their own countries with different badges. They would not be re-quired to act against their own nation but in other respects they would be directed by the world organization. This might be started on a modest scale and a grow [sic] as confidence grew. I wished to see this done after the First World War and trust it may be done forthwith.

Controlling the Atomic Bomb

It would nevertheless be wrong and imprudent to entrust the se-cret knowledge or experience of the atomic bomb, which the United States, Great Britain, and Canada now share, to the world organization, while it is still in its infancy. It would be criminal mad-ness to cast it adrift in this still agitated and un-united world. No one in any country has slept less well in their beds because this knowledge and the method and the raw materials to apply it are at present largely retained in American hands. I do not believe we should all have slept so soundly had the positions been reversed and some Communist or neo-Fascist state monopolized, for the time being, these dread agencies. The fear of them alone might easily have been used to enforce totalitarian systems upon the free dem-ocratic world, with consequences appalling to human imagination.

God has willed that this shall not be, and we have at least a breathing space before this peril has to be encountered, and even then, if no effort is spared, we should still possess so formidable a superiority as to impose effective deterrents upon its employment or threat of employment by others. Ultimately when the essential brother of man is truly embodied and expressed in a world orga-nization, these powers may be confided to it. . . .

There is . . . an important question we must ask ourselves. Would a special relationship between the United States and the British Commonwealth be inconsistent with our overriding loyalties to the world organization? I reply that on the contrary, it is probably the only means by which that organization will achieve its full stature and strength. There are already the special United States relations with Canada and between the United States and the South American republics. We also have our twenty years' treaty of collaboration and mutual assistance with Soviet Russia. I agree with Mr. Bevin that it might well be a fifty-year treaty. We have an alliance with Portugal unbroken since 1384. None of these clash with the general interest of a world agreement. On the contrary they help it. "In my Father's house are many mansions." Special associations between members of the United Nations which have no aggressive point against any other country, which harbor no design incompatible with the charter of the United Nations, far from being harmful, are beneficial and, as I believe, indispensable. . . .

A Shadow Has Fallen

A shadow has fallen upon the scenes so lately lighted by the Allied victory. Nobody knows what Soviet Russia and its Communist international organization intends to do in the immediate future, or what are the limits, if any, to their expansive and proselytizing tendencies. I have a strong admiration and regard for the valiant Russian people and for my wartime comrade, Marshal Stalin. There is sympathy and good will in Britain—and I doubt not here also—toward the peoples of all the Russias and a resolve to persevere through many differences and rebuffs in establishing lasting friendships.

We understand the Russian need to be secure on her western frontiers from all renewal of German aggression. We welcome her to her rightful place among the leading nations of the world. Above all, we welcome constant, frequent, and growing contacts between the Russian people and our own people on both sides of the Atlantic. It is my duty, however, to place before you certain facts about the present position in Europe.

An Iron Curtain Has Descended Across Europe

From Stettin in the Baltic to Trieste in the Adriatic, an iron curtain has descended across the continent. Behind that line lie all the capitals of the ancient states of Central and Eastern Europe. Warsaw, Berlin, Prague, Vienna, Budapest, Belgrade, Bucharest, and Sofia, all these famous cities and the populations around them lie in the Soviet sphere and all are subject, in one form or another, not only to Soviet influence but to a very high and increasing measure of control from Moscow. Athens alone, with its immortal glories, is free to decide its future at an election under British, American, and French observation.

The Russian-dominated Polish government has been encouraged to make enormous and wrongful inroads upon Germany, and mass expulsions of millions of Germans on a scale grievous and undreamed of are now taking place. The Communist parties, which were very small in all these eastern states of Europe, have been raised to preeminence and power far beyond their numbers and are seeking everywhere to obtain totalitarian control. Police governments are prevailing in nearly every case, and so far, except in Czechoslovakia, there is no true democracy.

Winston Churchill

Turkey and Persia are both profoundly alarmed and disturbed at the claims which are made upon them and at the pressure being exerted by the Moscow government. An attempt is being made by the Russians in Berlin to build up a quasi-Communist party in their zone of occupied Germany by showing special favors to groups of left-wing German leaders. At the end of the fighting last June, the American and British Armies withdrew westward, in accordance with an earlier agreement, to a depth at some points of 150 miles on a front of nearly 400 miles, to allow the Russians to occupy this vast expanse of territory which the Western democracies had conquered.

If now the Soviet government tries, by separate action, to build up a pro-Communist Germany in their areas, this will cause new serious difficulties in the British and American zones, and will give the defeated Germans the power of putting themselves up to auction between the Soviets and the Western democracies. Whatever conclusions may be drawn from these facts—and facts they are— this is certainly not the liberated Europe we fought to build up.

Nor is it one which contains the essentials of permanent peace.

In front of the iron curtain which lies across Europe are other causes for anxiety. In Italy the Communist party is seriously hampered by having to support the Communist-trained Marshall Tito's claims to former Italian territory at the head of the Adriatic. Nevertheless, the future of Italy hangs in the balance. Again, one cannot imagine a regenerated Europe without a strong France. . . .

However, in a great number of countries, far from the Russian frontiers and throughout the world, Communist fifth columns are established and work in complete unity and absolute obedience to the directions they receive from the Communist center. Except in the British Commonwealth, and in the United States, where communism is in its infancy, the Communist parties or fifth columns constitute a growing challenge and peril to Christian civilization. These are somber facts for anyone to have to recite on the morrow of a victory gained by so much splendid comradeship in arms and in the cause of freedom and democracy, and we should be most unwise not to face them squarely while time remains.

The Danger in Asia

The outlook is also anxious in the Far East and especially in Manchuria. The agreement which was made at Yalta, to which I was a party, was extremely favorable to Soviet Russia, but it was made at a time when no one could say that the German war might not extend all through the summer and autumn of 1945 and when the Japanese war was expected to last for a further eighteen months from the end of the German war. In this country you are all so well informed about the Far East and such devoted friends of China that I do not need to expatiate on the situation there.

I have felt bound to portray the shadow which, alike in the West and in the East, falls upon the world. I was a minister at the time of the Versailles Treaty and a close friend of Mr. Lloyd George. I did not myself agree with many things that were done, but I have a very strong impression in my mind of that situation, and I find it painful to contrast it with that which prevails now. In those days there were high hopes and unbounded confidence that the wars were over, and that the League of Nations would become all-powerful. I do not see or feel the same confidence or even the same hopes in the haggard world at this time.

On the other hand, I repulse the idea that a new war is inevitable, still more that it is imminent. It is because I am so sure that our fortunes are in our own hands and that we hold the power to save the future, that I feel the duty to speak out now that I have an occasion to do so. I do not believe that Soviet Russia desires war. What they desire is the fruits of war and the indefinite expansion of their power and doctrines. But what we have to consider here today while time remains, is the permanent prevention of war and the establishment of conditions of freedom and democracy as rapidly as possible in all countries.

We Must Avoid War

Our difficulties and dangers will not be removed by closing our eyes to them; they will not be removed by mere waiting to see what happens; nor will they be relieved by a policy of appeasement. What is needed is a settlement, and the longer this is delayed, the more difficult it will be and the greater our dangers will become. From what I have seen of our Russian friends and allies during the war, I am convinced that there is nothing they admire so much as strength, and there is nothing for which they have less respect than for military weakness. For that reason the old doctrine of a balance of power is unsound. We cannot afford, if we can help it, to work on narrow margins, offering temptations to a trial of strength. If the Western democracies stand together in strict adherence to the principles of the United Nations Charter, their influence for furthering these principles will be immense and no one is likely to molest them. If, however, they become divided or falter in their duty, and if these all-important years are allowed to slip away, then indeed catastrophe may overwhelm us all.

Last time I saw it all coming, and cried aloud to my own fellow countrymen and to the world, but no one paid any attention. Up till the year 1933 or even 1935, Germany might have been saved from the awful fate which has overtaken her and we might all have been spared the miseries Hitler let loose upon mankind.

There never was a war in all history easier to prevent by timely action than the one which has just desolated such great areas of the globe. It could have been prevented without the firing of a single shot, and Germany might be powerful, prosperous, and honored today, but no one would listen and one by one we were all sucked into the awful whirlpool.

We surely must not let that happen again. This can only be achieved by reaching now, in 1946, a good understanding on all points with Russia under the general authority of the United Nations and by the maintenance of that good understanding through many peaceful years, by the world instrument, supported by the whole strength of the English-speaking world and all its connections.

Let no man underrate the abiding power of the British Empire and Commonwealth. Because you see the 46 million in our island harassed about their food supply, of which they only grow one-half, even in wartime, or because we have difficulty in restarting our industries and export trade after six years of passionate war effort, do not suppose that we shall not come through these dark years of privations as we have come through the glorious years of agony, or that half a century from now, you will not see 70 or 80 millions of Britons spread about the world and united in defense of our traditions, our way of life, and of the world causes we and you espouse. If the population of the English-speaking commonwealth be added to that of the United States, with all that such cooperation implies in the air, on the sea, and in science and industry, there will be no quivering, precarious balance of power to offer its temptation to ambition or adventure. On the contrary there will be an overwhelming assurance of security. If we adhere faithfully to the charter of the United Nations and walk forward in sedate and sober strength, seeking no one's land or treasure, or seeking to lay no arbitrary control on the thoughts of men, if all British moral and material forces and convictions are joined with your own in fraternal association, the high roads of the future will be clear, not only for us but for all, not only for our time but for a century to come.

CHAPTER 3

How Did the Soviet Union Treat Its Citizens?

 **Chapter Preface**

When the Bolsheviks took power in Russia in 1917 they vowed to create an egalitarian society in which distinctions of birth, status, gender, and national origin would have no place. The equality espoused by the Communists was extended to all members of society. On paper, this equality was perfect. In reality, this equality was never achieved. The revolution and subsequent period of class warfare that dominated the Soviet Union in its early years eliminated the old privileged elites of the czarist system as well as the burgeoning middle class. But these changes did not completely eliminate inequality. In fact the new system led to the creation of a new elite. Some in the Soviet Union were clearly better off than others. Members of the Communist Party; the upper echelons of the government, the military, and other public institutions; and the cultural elite (as long as they toed the party line) all were afforded greater privilege than the common citizen. These elites were allowed to travel where others were not, given access to commodities that others were denied, and extended freedoms from which others were restricted. Thus the Communist goal of building an egalitarian society fell far short of the reality of Soviet life.

Gender equality was supposed to be inherent in the Soviet system, and indeed, women achieved many advances that would have been impossible in prerevolutionary Russia. Yet they were still treated as second-class citizens in many areas, and chauvinistic male attitudes proved difficult, if not impossible, to overcome. Although women were given ready access to divorce, abortion, and child care and were allowed opportunities to excel in the workplace and in professional fields, these measures did little to overturn deeply entrenched patriarchal attitudes. Soviet policies toward women became increasingly conservative over time. In the 1930s the divorce and abortion laws were repealed, and a conscious effort was begun to promote women's roles as mothers rather than as workers and professionals. Although women continued to work outside the home in many occupations, they were paid less than men. Nor were they able to obtain political or social prominence, as the highest levels of government and the Communist Party were virtually devoid of women. Despite the rhetoric of gender equality, women thus never achieved true parity with men under Soviet rule.

When the Bolsheviks came to power they also promised equality and autonomy to the various non-Russian nationalities that lived within the borders of the Soviet Union. Many such groups had supported the Bolsheviks precisely because they represented an end to the mistreatment they had suffered under the czarist empire. Yet these national groups never obtained these rights. Instead, their national aspirations were suppressed and Russian language and culture was imposed upon them by the Soviet regime. Most of the non-Russian republics of the USSR were consistently neglected, politically and economically, by the center in Moscow. Some were even forcibly relocated to suit the needs of the empire and its ethnically Russian inhabitants. As a result, growing discontent with the Soviet regime on the part of the non-Russian nationalities was a significant factor in the ultimate demise of the Soviet Union in 1991.

Viewpoint 1

"The young Soviet state adopted legislation ensuring full equality of women with men in all spheres of life."

Women Have Full Equal Rights and Opportunities Under Soviet Rule

Anonymous

One of the major goals of Russian Marxists was equality of all people, including women. Therefore, after the revolution women were granted complete legal rights and equality and guaranteed the same opportunities as men, at least on paper. Women were supposed to be full and equal partners in the building of socialism, which would relieve them of the drudgery of household labor. The new government undertook a variety of efforts aimed at improving women's lives and relieving them of what Soviet leader Vladimir I. Lenin termed "domestic slavery." In this article, written in the 1970s, official Soviet researchers assert that women have achieved many advances through the progressive policies of the Communist party and government. Soviet women, they contend, have benefited greatly from the

Anonymous, *Women in the Soviet Union: Statistical Returns*. Moscow: Progress Publishers, 1970.

campaign to educate women and bring them into the work-force, which has resulted in widespread literacy among women and a dramatic increase in the percentage of female workers. The government has granted women equal pay with men, estab-lished day care facilities to help women with child care, made extended maternity leave available to all female workers, and le-galized abortion and divorce. The authors also point to the nu-merous women who have become leaders in various fields of in-dustry, science, culture, and politics.

After the victory of the Great October Socialist Revolution, which removed the power of capitalists and landowners from the face of Russia, the young Soviet state adopted legislation en-suring full equality of women with men in all spheres of life. For the first time in history women were accorded genuine rights: to elect and be elected to organs of power, the right to work, to equal pay and education, property and parental rights on an equal foot-ing with men.

The new legal status of women contributed a great deal to es-tablishing genuine equality of men and women. The problem was to be solved along lines advocated by Lenin, the founder of the So-viet state. Lenin believed that women had to be drawn into socially productive work and state administration, that they had to be re-leased from "domestic slavery" and that conditions had to be cre-ated for helping mothers to bring up their children.

Women's Status in Pre-Revolutionary Russia

In pre-revolutionary Russia 80 per cent of all employed women worked as domestic servants and farm-labourers, 13 per cent at enterprises and building-sites and only 4 per cent in education and public health. 83.4 per cent of women between the age of 9 and 49 were illiterate. Women were excluded from receiving edu-cation in any way possible.

The status of women was particularly grim and their rights par-ticularly meagre in the eastern regions of tsarist Russia where un-der the influence of age-old traditions and the demands of religious dogmata women were isolated from society, lived the life of a recluse and were entirely dependent upon their husbands.

The Advance Brought by the Revolution

As soon as it came into being the Soviet state under the leadership of the Communist Party drew up a broad programme for the emancipation of women. A gigantic scheme to eliminate illiteracy was undertaken with similar schemes to train qualified women specialists and to give women general and specialised education. The conditions were being created for women to combine social life and work with motherhood and family duties: the state organised a mother-and-child welfare system and built pre-school and out-of-school institutions for children.

Backward and reactionary views on women were gradually overcome.

In a comparatively short historical period, as socialist society has been built, Soviet woman has become a real member of society who enjoys full rights. This is one of the most remarkable achievements of socialism. Soviet women deserve great credit for the success achieved in building socialist and communist society in the U.S.S.R. . . .

Women in the Workforce

Women in the U.S.S.R. make full use of their right to work. About 50 per cent of the population engaged in social production are women. There are whole economic and cultural fields, such as education, public health, trade and public catering, where women predominate.

Mechanisation and automation of production, which have taken the drudgery out of work, ample opportunities for receiving general and special education, professional training and improved qualifications have enabled women to work in a wide variety of branches of the national economy. . . .

Women are taking a more and more active part in production management accounting for more than a third of all workers with senior and specialised posts in industry. 58 per cent of all specialists with higher or secondary special education, engaged in the national economy, are women and every third engineer is a woman. . . .

Women in the Sciences and Culture

Women work successfully in scientific and cultural fields accounting for more than a third of all research workers. Many women have won world recognition by their work, like Pelageya Kochina, academician and a leading authority on hydromechanics and the theory of filtration; Olga Bazilevskaya, a physicist at the Kurchatov Institute of Atomic Energy and Lenin Prize laureate; Maria Nadirova, senior scientific worker at the Azerbaijan Institute of Petro-chemical Processes and State Prize laureate; Lidia Jakobson, professor of microbiology, and Valentina Mamontova, selectionist, Hero of Socialist Labour and Lenin Prize laureate. Professor Alla Masevich, doctor of physico-mathematical sciences, is vice-president of the Astronomical Counsil at the U.S.S.R. Academy of Sciences and heads the Artificial Earth Satellite Tracking Service.

Valentina Nikolayeva-Tereshkova, Hero of the Soviet Union and first woman cosmonaut, made a considerable contribution to the study of outer space. In the space-craft "Vostok-6" she orbited the earth 48 times while fulfilling a complex research programme.

In the Soviet period a whole galaxy of outstanding women writers, poets, artists, actresses and composers have made their appearance on the cultural scene. People in the Soviet Union and abroad are well acquainted with the writers Marietta Shaginyan and Vera Panova, the poetesses Margarita Aliger and Zulfia Israilova, the sculptress Vera Mukhina, the artist Tatyana Yablonskaya, the composer Alexandra Pakhmutova, the conductor Veronika Dudarova, the ballerinas Galina Ulanova and Maya Plisetskaya, the singers Galina Vishnevskaya and Goar Gasparyan.

Women in Social and Political Life

Women play a prominent part in the social and political life of the country and in state administration. In 1966, 425 women or 28 per cent of all deputies were elected to the Supreme Soviet of the U.S.S.R. Hundreds of thousands of women have been elected deputies to Supreme Soviets of the Union and Autonomous republics and local Soviets. . . .

Women work as members of the Government of the U.S.S.R. and governments of the Union republics. Twenty-seven women are ministers in the Union republics. Yekaterina Furtseva has long held the post of Minister of Culture of the U.S.S.R.

Women take an active part in the work of public organisations. They account for almost a half of all Soviet trade union members and take a great deal of the work on their shoulders. Two and a half million women are members of the C.P.S.U. [Communist Party of the Soviet Union].

In the U.S.S.R. there is no discrimination whatever with regard to women. They are employed and accepted at places of learning on an equal footing with men and the principle of equal pay for equal work is strictly observed.

Women's Special Protection Under the Law

Considering the physiological peculiarities of the female organism and in the interests of safeguarding the health of mothers and children, Soviet legislation forbids employment of women in certain kinds of harmful and heavy work (underground work and certain other kinds in the chemical, printing, metallurgical industries, etc.).

Like men, Soviet women have the right to recreation: they are granted annual paid holidays and have a wide network of sanatoria, holiday homes, tourist centres, mountaineering camps and stadiums at their disposal. In order to create favourable conditions for the normal development of children and to safeguard the health of mothers, pregnant women are granted a special paid leave during pregnancy and childbirth: 56 days before childbirth and 56 days after in excess of their annual holiday. In the event of complications during delivery or the birth of twins post-natal leave is raised to 70 days. So that a child can be fed at the proper time, paid breaks after every three and a half hours lasting not less than half an hour are granted to working women supplementary to normal lunch breaks. After the post-natal rest period a mother may take extra unpaid leave of up to three months, in which case her place of work and former position are reserved for her. If after childbirth a woman spends a year away from work she is still entitled to continuity of service.

An extensive network of maternity and infant health centres cares for the health of expectant mothers and then their children. Every Soviet woman, whether she lives in town or country, has the opportunity to bear her child in a maternity home. Obstetric assistance, care and feeding in hospital are available free like all medical services in the U.S.S.R.

The Soviet state accepts a considerable share of the care for children's health and upbringing. A comprehensive system of pre-school and out-of-school institutions has been organised throughout the Soviet Union. At the present time more than 8 million children attend kindergartens and nurseries. By 1970 the number of places in pre-school institutions will be able to cater for 12.2 million children.

Viewpoint 2

"Despite . . . the enormous propaganda hoopla about women in the Soviet media, Soviet women remain a distinctly second sex."

Women Do Not Have Full Equal Rights and Opportunities Under Soviet Rule

Hedrick Smith

Despite the fact that women were officially granted full equal rights and opportunities in the Soviet Union, women still faced numerous difficulties after the revolution. In this viewpoint written in the 1970s, Hedrick Smith, Pulitzer prize–winning journalist for the *New York Times* and fellow at the Johns Hopkins University School of Advanced Studies, details the burdens placed on Soviet women at the time and the obstacles they faced in achieving true equality. Smith demonstrates that male chauvinism is deeply ingrained in Russian culture and these attitudes prove very difficult to overcome. Furthermore, he asserts, although a great number of women are given opportunities to work outside the home, they are still expected to perform all do-

Hedrick Smith, *The Russians*. New York: Quadrangle/The New York Times Book Company, 1976. Copyright © 1976 by Hedrick Smith. Reproduced by permission.

91

mestic chores and childrearing. Therefore, they have a "double burden," wherein they have to work a full day at their jobs outside the home, only to return in the evening to face the cooking, cleaning, and child care. Women have entered a number of professions from which they have previously been excluded. In fact, in some professions, such as medicine, the number of women surpasses that of men. Smith points out, however, that instead of achieving prestige and higher wages as a result of their participation in these professions, the professions themselves have come to be seen as "women's work" and are therefore devalued. Moreover, Smith asserts that most Soviet women have to work out of financial necessity rather than the desire for professional achievement or fiscal independence.

L ong ago the Stalinist constitution of 1936 declared [women's] "equal rights with men in all spheres of economic, state, cultural, public and political life" which American women's libbers were still battling to get added to the American Constitution in the mid-Seventies. On paper, Soviet women already have it made. They are officially liberated. Abortions are legal. Four-month paid maternity leaves are written into law, and jobs must be kept for new mothers for a year. A network of state-subsidized day-care centers has been set up nationwide and cares for ten million preschoolers. Equal pay for equal work is established as a principle. A higher proportion of Soviet women work than in any other industrialized country and a modest number have achieved career successes. Vast numbers have completed higher education and work beside men in science, industry and government.

Women Still Face Many Problems

Yet despite these achievements and the enormous propaganda hoopla about women in the Soviet media, Soviet women remain a distinctly second sex. If any large segment of the population has been exploited by the system, it is women. Even three decades after World War II, when educated urban women are watching their figures, chasing Western fashions and worrying more about their femininity than Russian women ever found time to do in the past, women still do the bulk of the low-paying, backbreaking, dirty manual labor. They shoulder a wearisome double burden of work plus what Lenin termed "domestic slavery." Justifiably, they complain of inadequate relief from the competing tensions of career and family.

From afar or on hurried visits to the Soviet Union where they have met occasional feminine successes like Mariya Fyodorovna, some American women speak enviously of their Soviet counterparts. But life looks different up close. No American woman I encountered who had lived among Russians long enough to have a genuine feel for what their lives entail, would think of swapping places. The main reason, as Russian women themselves say, is that contrary to Lenin's dictum, mass access to the job market has not proven the panacea that either Lenin or some Western feminists presumed. In many ways, it has made life more trying. Some Russian women even feel so disadvantaged that one confided candidly to an American woman I knew: "I hope my child is a boy, not a girl. As a boy, his life would be so much easier."

In spite of the declared Marxist-Leninist commitment to feminine equality, the strong tradition of male chauvinism in Russian life has been only mildly moderated by the Soviets. The enduring assumptions of male superiority and feminine subservience come through in Russian humor, so often revealing of deep-set attitudes. . . .

Not long before I left for Moscow, an American woman of Russian descent gave me a couple of booklets of Russian proverbs. I was surprised at the blatant male chauvinism, in a number of them: "A wife isn't a jug—she won't crack if you hit her a few"; "When you take an eel by its tail or a woman by her word, there's precious little stays in your hands"; or "A dog is wiser than a woman—he won't bark at his master." Working-class women nowadays still take rough drinking and rough handling from their menfolk very much for granted. . . .

Women in the Workforce

[The] male vacuum of the immediate postwar period drew millions of women into the economy and was the springboard toward success for some of today's middle-aged women. Women now account for nearly one-fourth of the Soviet equivalent of Ph.D's, close to one-third of the ordinary judges, nearly one-third of the 1,517 members of the Supreme Soviet (parliament), about 70 percent of the doctors, and about 15,000 members of the professional unions of journalists, writers, artists, architects, composers and film workers. More than five million women have had some higher education, not too much of a lag behind the men. In part, this is a result of the lopsided feminine majority in the population after the war. Yet even as peacetime birth rates have begun to even out the Soviet population and build up the male share, the government has kept up intensive recruiting to draw every possible woman out of the household into the labor force. Women are actually a larger proportion of the work force today than in 1950. During the 1960's, more than 16 million additional women were put in jobs—a staggering figure. Even though the rate of growth slowed in the Seventies as the reservoir of unemployed women was depleted, roughly 60 million women were at work in 1974, close to 85 percent of all working-age women, the highest percentage in the industrialized world (in America the figure was just about 50 percent).

Most Soviet women by now take a job as part of the natural order of things and find it hard to imagine not working. So strongly ingrained in them is the work-ethic that there is a stigma to being simply a housewife. . . .

Yet for all this, it is basically the economic imperatives—both for the government and the individual—which really leave Soviet women no alternative but to work. Most of the day-care centers and other supporting institutions which Soviet propagandists so constantly ascribe to the state's benign solicitude for feminine liberation are actually indispensable requirements for keeping as many women as possible on the job. Several Russian women commented rather bitterly that the network of state nurseries, kindergartens and children's summer camps were less to aid their selffulfillment than the fulfillment of production norms at the factory. Indeed, Western economists have noted that a fair share of the Soviet economic growth over the past 15 years has come through increasing the size of the labor force, especially by getting more women—and pensioners—to work.

On a personal level, few Soviet families could enjoy the luxury of having only one parent at work. Most fathers earn too little (average factory workers' pay in 1974 was $187 monthly) to support a family of three, let alone four or more. One of the most persistent reactions to American life that I encountered among Russians was their surprise that large numbers of American families could be supported by the father alone. Even middle-class Russians, who were my counterparts in Soviet society, were incredulous that in a family of six, my wife did not have to work to contribute to the family budget. Finances in Russian families with children are often so touch-and-go even with both parents working that some women do not even use all the unpaid maternity leave to which they are legally entitled because their families cannot afford to live on the husband's salary alone. I knew one couple where the husband, a government worker, made a good salary of about $350 a month, yet his wife went back to work after only nine months maternity leave because they felt a financial squeeze. For the overwhelming majority of urban women, the practical choice of not working simply does not exist. . . .

Women in Public Life

In their careers, many Soviet women complain of discrimination just as vehemently as Western women. Superficially, this may seem surprising because women are so visible in Soviet public life. For Soviet politicians are just as sensitive to a show of "ticket-balancing" as American politicians are and usually arrange to have women's representatives or women's delegates prominently placed at any public occasion. Propagandists never tire of boasting about Soviet women in figurehead positions, disregarding the reality that men really run things. The press, for example, brags frequently that more women sit in the Supreme Soviet "than in all the parliaments of the capitalist states combined." But this is a spurious comparison. The Supreme Soviet is for show, a sweetener for women (or minority nationalities) that often misleads foreigners. It is a rubber-stamp body that has unanimously approved every single measure put to it.

Within the Communist Party, the real apparatus of power, Soviet women have fared no better and probably not as well as

American women in the political life of their country. Not one of the 15 members of the ruling Politburo, which makes all the key decisions, is a woman. Nor is there any woman among the nine national secretaries in the Party Secretariat, which runs the day-to-day operations of the Party. Half a dozen women are members of the powerful 241-member Party Central Committee, a proportion slightly smaller than the number of women in Congress (though a couple of these women were token representatives of labor rather than people of real power, as most Central Committee members are). Like America, the Soviet Union has notably lagged behind countries such as India, Israel, Ceylon or Great Britain which have put women at the head of their governments or a major political party. In roughly six decades of Soviet power, the one woman who made it into the Politburo was Yekaterina Furtseva, a favorite of Khrushchev who was soon demoted but served from 1960 until she died in 1974 as the only woman in the Soviet Cabinet. Even at Republic and provincial levels, almost no women have risen to positions of command. America may have had only four women governors, but no women have had comparable posts of power as Party bosses of a Republic or a major province. Occasionally in Russia, as in the West, the inbred unselfconscious male chauvinism comes out in embarrassing ways, but none during my tour topped the official announcement of the Soviet Commission for International Women's Year in 1975—headed by a man.

Women Do the Work

In the economy, the picture for women is better but not a great deal. Khrushchev, in a candid observation to a large meeting of agricultural supervisors, is supposed to have surveyed the scene and remarked disapprovingly that "it turns out that it is the men who do the administering and the women who do the work." Women do comprise roughly half the work force in industry, yet nine out of ten plant managers are men. Women represent nearly half of those engaged in scientific work but only ten percent of the senior professors or members of the Academy of Sciences. Close to three-fourths of Soviet schoolteachers are women but three-fourths of the principals in the basic eight- and ten-grade schools are men. About 70 percent of the doctors are women but men get the lion's share of the prestigious jobs as top surgeons, department supervisors or hospital directors. Those figures may not compare too unfavorably with the West, but given the numbers of women in the Russian work force, they do undercut the contention that Moscow is far ahead in granting women equality.

In Russia, equal pay for equal work is an accepted principle, but getting the equal work is the problem. Millions of women are shunted into the lower-paying, less prestigious fields. Teaching and medicine are prime examples. These are practically at the bottom of the pay and status scales and these are the professions in which women are most heavily represented. In industry, women work mostly in the light, consumer sector where, according to Soviet studies, pay and all other benefits are well below those in heavy industry (where men predominate). In farming, women provide the core of the low-paid, unskilled field hands while men operate the machinery and get better pay. Perhaps most indicative of the situation nationwide, one major Soviet economic study drafting a working-class family budget assumed that the husband would earn 50 percent more than the wife. . . .

Moreover, as a schoolteacher commented to me bitterly, "In Russia, women do the dog's work"—the grubby, low-paying work that in America is consigned to blacks and wetbacks. Indeed, most Western tourists arriving in Russia for the first time are forcibly struck by Russian women cracking asphalt on the highways and hefting shovelfuls into trucks (while the male truckdriver watches), using crowbars to pry loose old railroad ties, sweeping streets or shoveling snow and cracking ice in winter, carrying hod, hoeing potato fields, slapping paint on buildings in the coldest weather, or heaving coal onto trains along the Trans-Siberian Railroad. "How can one fail to feel shame and compassion at the sight of our women carrying heavy barrows of stones for paving the street?" Aleksandr Solzhenitsyn asked in his open letter to the leadership before he was exiled. Some Soviet officials privately share the embarrassment of having women work like beasts of burden, but many Russians are not shocked by it because it has been so long part of their scene.

Finally, the financial imperative to work and the chaotic inefficiency of consumer life puts the working Russian woman in a crucible that very few American women experience and that Soviet welfare programs only partially relieve. Soviet women find themselves inescapably mortgaged to two worlds: work and family. Unable to succeed in either they are left to race, as one Soviet writer put it, like "squirrels in a cage."

Viewpoint 3

"Only socialism can provide real freedom—freedom for all."

The People of the Soviet Union Are Free

Vladimir Denisov

The democratic countries of the West tended to look at the Communist systems in Eastern Europe as fundamentally opposed to freedom due to their restrictions on civil liberties. But Communists did not define freedom in entirely the same way as people in the West. In the following viewpoint Vladimir Denisov, deputy editor in chief of the Soviet Novosti Press Agency during the 1960s, presents the Communist view of freedom. He argues that freedom from hunger, cold, and material needs is much more pressing for human happiness than are civil liberties. Denisov contends that socialism is the only system that provides for these necessities, therefore making it the only system that can truly assure human beings real freedom. Under socialism, he asserts, all people are equal and have equal access to all services and opportunities, a further condition of true freedom. Moreover, it is socialism, he argues, that allows people to enjoy their labor instead of being forced to work for their survival as under capitalism. The advancements brought about by socialism also allow people greater freedom for creative endeavors and for recreation, according to Denisov.

Vladimir Denisov, *Communism Stands for Freedom.* London: Soviet Booklets, 1962.

> *Capitalism is the road of suffering for the people. . . . Socialism*
> *is the road to freedom and happiness for the people.*
> FROM THE PROGRAMME OF THE C.P.S.U.
> [Communist Party of the Soviet Union]

The future of mankind depends on the outcome of the competition taking place in the world of today between the two social systems—socialism and capitalism. Victory in this contest will go to the social system that provides men and women with the greatest material and spiritual advantages, creates real conditions for the full development of the human personality, and establishes a real "kingdom of freedom".

What Is Freedom?

> *The entire life of socialist society is based on the principle of*
> *broad democracy. . . . Socialist democracy includes both politi-*
> *cal freedom—freedom of speech, of the press and of assembly, the*
> *right to elect and to be elected, and also social rights—the right*
> *to work, to rest and leisure, to free education and free medical*
> *services, to material security in old age and in case of illness or*
> *disability; equality of citizens of all races and nationalities; equal*
> *rights for women and men in all spheres of political, economic*
> *and cultural activity. Socialist democracy, unlike bourgeois*
> *democracy, does not merely proclaim the rights of the people, but*
> *guarantees that they are really implemented.*
> FROM THE PROGRAMME OF THE C.P.S.U.

When people in Western countries read these lines in the Programme of the Soviet Communist Party, they may object that all political parties talk about freedom. The United States describes itself as the "free world" and the "champion" of freedom. But communists reject what the capitalists call freedom. They declare that only socialism can provide real freedom—freedom for all.

Which is right?

History has already given the answer.

Communists do not only promise freedom in their Programme. They also explain what they mean by freedom. And—what is perhaps the best argument—the Soviet Communists, who were the first in the world to build socialism and have now set about building communism, have shown in practice that the new social system liberates working people from all forms of oppression and exploitation, and provides the most favourable social conditions for every man and woman to obtain real, tangible and not merely formal opportunities for free and all-round development.

Man has today achieved such a level of maturity that people no longer acquiesce in the absence or limitation of freedom. "Life without liberty is worthless," said Romain Rolland, the great French writer. Mankind possesses no prouder or more sacred word than "freedom". The history of mankind is the history of the struggle for liberation.

Many great sacrifices have been made for the cause of freedom. But its universal triumph has yet to be achieved. There are still nations fettered by the chains of colonialism.

Hunger and poverty still threaten the lives and health of certain sections of the population in many parts of the world, even in economically advanced countries. Scientists have invented many miraculous medicines—but epidemics still flare up, killing or crippling many people. Millions of families still live in slums.

Can large-scale unemployment, the lack of opportunities for young people to get an education or a trade, the banning of progressive political parties and the peace movement supporters, or the disfranchisement of large sections of the population for reasons of colour or property qualifications—all to be found in the capitalist world—be considered compatible with "freedom"?

In the light of such facts, how is one to understand freedom? What is it that freedom should give to the individual and to society as a whole? Where is the borderline between genuine and false liberty, between freedom for the few and freedom for all?

The Foundation of Freedom

The rights and liberties of citizens may be solemnly proclaimed in a country's constitution, which describes those rights and liberties as "inalienable" and "natural". But is it sufficient to possess a right in order to enjoy it? The formal possession of a right is not enough; it must be confirmed materially. Otherwise, equality means merely formal equality in the eyes of the law, while man's actual status in society is determined solely by his wealth. . . . Society can give its members genuine freedom only if it can first and foremost guarantee their material welfare and economic independence. The degree to which any society is free is indicated by the material foundations of the freedom it extends to its citizens. . . .

Working people, who make up the vast majority of society, . . . need . . . first and foremost, freedom from want and oppression, freedom from fear for the morrow and for the future of their children. That is the principal freedom, the foundation of genuine economic and social freedom for the mass of the people. "Freedom of speech, of ideas and of conscience can acquire significance only given the freedom to live. . . . Therefore to judge whether or not freedom exists in a given society, it is first of all necessary to see whether there is unemployment there, how people are ensured the means of existence, how social security is given effect, and whether life is maladjusted. . . . If the basic freedoms are not provided in a society, it cannot, in essence, be considered free, no matter how many non-basic freedoms are provided," writes the Japanese philosopher Yanagida Kenzuro.

The most extensive and lavishly proclaimed freedom is worthless unless it has a material basis. Under such "freedom" man has only two alternatives—to fall into line, or starve.

The yardstick of genuine freedom is the existence of the economic basis necessary for the unhampered enjoyment of freedom by every member of society. . . .

Liberated Labour—The Foundation of All Freedoms

Our socialist society is a united family of working people enjoying equal rights. Wealth, national origin, or position are neither privileges nor obstacles to a Soviet man. All Soviet people have equal rights and at the same time are in duty bound to work according to their abilities, and are paid according to the work done.

For whom do Soviet workers, peasants, or intellectuals work? It is with a sense of pride that every Soviet citizen can reply, and say that he is working for himself, for his family, and for the welfare of society as a whole. It cannot be otherwise, for under socialism each man's place of employment is the property of the people as a whole. . . .

The abolition of private property and the transfer of all the wealth of society to the people as a whole as publicly-owned property means not only that each individual is freed from exploitation and oppression, but also the emancipation of all society from the anarchy of production, economic crises and other ruinous phenomena inherent in the capitalist system.

Some Western sociologists like to depict the unorganised, chaotic nature of the capitalist economy as almost the supreme manifestation of freedom. But it is common knowledge that "private enterprise" has long been a fiction, not only because so much wealth is required to take advantage of that freedom—wealth which no man can earn by his own labour—but also because the monopolies that now dominate almost all branches of the capitalist economy prevent any freedom of enterprise.

The scientific organisation of the socialist economy on the basis of over-all plans for the national economy has opened up great prospects for the development of the productive forces, the advancement of science and technology, and the continuous growth of social wealth and consequently of the well-being of all. . . .

Under socialism, the whole of society has become free in the deepest and fullest sense of the word; consequently each member of society enjoys genuine freedom—freedom for all cannot but mean freedom for each. It cannot be otherwise, for a genuinely civilised society can have no aims other than those of the individuals that go to make up that society. It is only by serving each man and giving effect to his aspirations that society justifies its purpose. Socialist society is that sort of society, because it has created conditions in which each individual enjoys unlimited opportunities for the development of his abilities and the satisfaction of his ever-growing needs. These conditions include, above all, the guaranteed right to work and leisure, free education and medical aid, the steady reduction of working hours and the wide development of housing and cultural development. . . .

Freed from dependence on the will and whims of private owners, Soviet workers have legal and other guarantees of employment. The Soviet citizen does not have to accept just any kind of work to support himself and his family. "Situations vacant" notices for jobs of all kinds are to be seen outside factories and elsewhere. . . .

Vocational Training and Leisure Time

One of the most important conditions for the free development of the individual that socialism provides is the opportunity for all to acquire a skill or profession in accordance with their interests and inclinations. Our system of education and vocational training, free and therefore accessible to all, is in the forefront of the Soviet state's attention. The desire to acquire knowledge and improve qualifications and education in every way is encouraged. . . . Study and the improvement of the cultural level of the masses is not only highly beneficial to society as a whole, it is also a most important means of raising the political consciousness and activity of each individual, whose creative possibilities and fields of interest are broadened in consequence. . . .

There is also another rung in the ladder of freedom—the ever greater leisure provided by the reduction of working hours. Man's life is not limited to work alone: he needs rest and leisure for self-education and recreation. . . .

Technological advances and higher labour productivity make it possible for socialist society constantly to reduce working hours. Within the next ten years Soviet factory and office workers will go over to a six-hour day—five hours in mines and occupations injurious to health. Then during the following ten years working hours will be still further reduced, and the Soviet Union will become a country with the shortest, most productive and best paid working day in the world. Workers will have considerably more free time for rest, studies, sport, cultural activities and travelling. This reduction in working hours will be accompanied by a rise in standards of living. Thus, science and engineering, which under socialism are directed towards peaceful and creative ends, become a most important factor contributing to emancipation of the individual, to his physical and intellectual development.

Free labour is a source of joy and pleasure. The life of Soviet people is steeped in this atmosphere. The worker who engages in emulation with his comrades and at the same time helps them, the innovator who introduces an efficiency proposal and helps to secure its wide application in production, the inventor of new machines which help boost productivity and make work easier—all these are genuinely creative individuals in the new and genuinely free communist world. Freedom from want in socialist society means not only economic, material freedom, but also spiritual freedom, since it emancipates man from oppressive fears and worries, and is a source of optimism and enthusiasm. . . .

The Kingdom of Freedom

The Soviet Communist Party's new Programme sets an historic aim—that of . . . securing the complete satisfaction of the material and cultural needs of each man and woman.

With the achievement of the aims set by the Soviet Communist Party's Programme as regards the improvement of the material welfare of the people, the Soviet Union will make considerable strides towards the implementation of the communist principle of distribution according to need. The transition to distribution according to need will mean emancipation, it will signify each man's complete liberation from all material cares, and equal opportunities for all to devote their powers and abilities to creative labour.

On the basis of advanced science and technology, the maximum productivity of labour, an abundance of all kinds of foodstuffs, and the elimination of any distinctions between mental and physical labour, between life in towns and in the countryside, man in communist society will be fully emancipated from slavish dependence on the caprices of Nature. Communism will, in fact, mean a tremendous leap from the "kingdom of necessity" into the "kingdom of freedom", in which the individual will have unlimited opportunities to display his abilities and talents in any field.

This society of freedom has already set out upon its triumphant march. Its outline can be distinctly traced in Soviet life today.

The Communist Party of the Soviet Union has solemnly proclaimed that the present generation of Soviet people will live under communism!

Viewpoint 4

"Where communism prevails, faith, freedom, morality, and religion wither."

The People of the Soviet Union Are Not Free

Ezra Taft Benson

In this viewpoint, written in the 1960s during the height of Cold War tensions between the Soviet Union and the United States, Ezra Taft Benson, U.S. secretary of agriculture under President Dwight D. Eisenhower, asserts that there can be no freedom under communism. He paints a dark picture of the Communist system, wherein complete control of the citizenry's daily life is maintained by a sinister, even "evil" government. He maintains that life under Communist rule is severely restricted; property is state owned and decisions about daily life are dictated from above. There is no freedom to speak one's mind, to worship as one pleases, to belong to the organizations one chooses, or even to decide where to live or work, according to Benson. Moreover, he asserts that such a system seeks to actively destroy all elements of freedom in the world. He does not, however, blame the Russian people for their oppressive conditions, but rather their totalitarian government and the Communist Party.

Ezra Taft Benson, *The Red Carpet*. Salt Lake City: Bookcraft, 1962.

All over the world the light of freedom is being diminished. Across whole continents of the earth freedom is being totally obliterated.

Never in recorded history has any movement spread its power so far and so fast as has socialistic-communism in the last three decades. The facts are not pleasant to review. Communist leaders are jubilant with their success. They are driving freedom back on almost every front.

We are in the midst of continuing international crisis—crisis constantly being stirred up by communist world expansion. The outlook for world peace and security is dark indeed. The gravity of the world situation is increasing daily. The United Nations seem unable to settle the troubles of the world. In truth we are faced with the hard fact that the United Nations, now largely dominated by communist countries, their sympathizers and the so-called neutrals, seems to have largely failed in its purpose. Yes, the days ahead are sobering and challenging. . . .

A deadly conflict between good and evil is constantly going on in the world. Some people may try to gloss it over, but the fact remains that one-third of the world's people live in the grip of a political and philosophical system that is truly diabolical.

We must never forget exactly what communism is. Communism is far more than an economic system. It is a total philosophy of life—atheistic and materialistic and utterly and completely opposed to all that we hold dear as a free and God-fearing people.

Where communism prevails, faith, freedom, morality, and religion wither.

The major communist objective, make no mistake about it, is to destroy any society that adheres to the fundamentals of spiritual, economic and political freedom—the integrity of man. . . .

What Life Would Be Like Under Communism

Suppose for a moment that this country fell under communist control. What would be the fruits of this calamity? First, the true seat of government would immediately be removed from Washington to Moscow. William Z. Foster, the former head of the Communist Party in the United States, said this: "When a communist heads the government of the United States—and that day will come just as surely as the sun rises—the government will not be a capitalistic government but a Soviet government, and behind this government will stand the Red Army to enforce the dictatorship of the proletariat."

What would this mean to you and me in our daily lives?

Could you own your own homes? Your living quarters would be assigned to you and you would pay rent to the state as ordered.

The farms of America are famed world wide. Most of them have been family owned and operated for two centuries. Under communism could you own your own farms? Your farms would be collectivized and become the property of the state and you would work them under orders from the state. You would be moved off the land into community centers or communes, and you would go out from there to work the fields—not YOUR fields, mind you, but the state's. This is what has happened in Russia, China and other communist nations.

Could you start a business and hire people to work for you? To do so would make you criminals.

Could you work where you pleased? You would work when,

For families like this one in Novosibrisk, Russia, living under Communist rule can restrict their daily-life freedoms such as where they may live and work.

where, and how you were told—and the government would do the telling. No farm organizations, chambers of commerce, labor unions, Rotary, Elks, and similar organizations as we now know them would be permitted to exist.

What would happen to your bank accounts? All above a small sum would be confiscated. The rest would be state-controlled for you. The state would take over your insurance.

Except for a few closely personal items, you would have no property to leave to your families when you die.

You could travel around the country only with police permission.

You could not travel abroad or marry a foreigner without the specific approval of the state.

You could not even write freely to friends in other countries.

Under communism our private colleges would cease to exist. Our children would go to the schools selected for them, and only so long as the state permitted. Lenin said, "give us a child for eight years and it will be a Bolshevik forever."

Teachers would be free to teach only what the state authorized. Foster said, "Our teachers must write new school textbooks and rewrite history from the Marxian viewpoint."

To belong to a church would be sure to bring discrimination and penalties of many kinds against you and your families. The great majority of church buildings would become state museums or warehouses. . . .

Life Behind the Iron Curtain

I have been behind the Iron Curtain. There the American visitor gets a strange feeling—an awareness of the fear of the people when they live under the totalitarian shadow of oppression.

I have been asked if, based on my experience and travels across this country and to countries behind the Iron Curtain, do I still hold the same views on the importance of freedom that I did when I first became Secretary of Agriculture.

I certainly do. Perhaps with an even stronger conviction after visiting Russia and the other communist-run countries. . . .

Everywhere there is tragedy and despair resulting from their loss of freedom. It was heart-rending to see people who had lost not only their worldly possessions but their God-given freedom.

Now why is this so. It is not because the Russian people are not good people. I found it easy to love them. My heart went out to them. Generally speaking they have about the same desires in their hearts as we have. They love their families, they love their homes, they want to raise their standard of living and do what is right. They want to live at peace with their neighbors. They want to be brothers with all mankind.

A Diabolical System

But the Russian people are operating under a diabolical system which is economically, socially and spiritually unsound and which cannot produce the fruits that can be produced under a system of freedom.

This communistic, totalitarian system is forced upon the Russian people by their Marxist-Leninist masters exercising the powers of a police state. Our visit to Russia was moving beyond any description—because it evidenced the tragedy and hardship that follow when individuals become pawns of the state. What we saw behind the Iron Curtain left us more deeply impressed than ever before with the privileges and blessings of freedom. There is darkness behind the Iron Curtain. It is indeed a world of suffering, despair, slave-labor camps, fear, betrayal, and lost human rights.

Viewpoint 5

"How can one justify the imprisonment . . . of persons who are oppositionists but whose opposition is still within legal bounds?"

The Soviet Union Needs the Voices of Dissent

Andrei D. Sakharov, with Valentin F. Turchin and Roy A. Medvedev

Andrei D. Sakharov was a brilliant physicist who was instrumental in developing the atomic bomb in the Soviet Union. For many years he worked in secrecy on the most highly classified projects for the Soviet government. In the late 1950s and early 1960s, however, Sakharov began to contemplate humanitarian issues and began speaking out against nuclear weapons. He also began to criticize the policies of the Soviet government and called for an end to censorship, human rights violations, political imprisonment, and other restrictions on the Soviet population. He soon paid a price for his political activity, losing his security clearance, then his job and the many benefits he had received. But these consequences did not stop him from continuing to speak out against the injustices of Soviet society. In this document, a manifesto issued in 1970, Sakharov, along with fel-

Andrei D. Sakharov, with Valentin F. Turchin and Roy A. Medvedev, "Manifesto II (A Joint Letter to the Central Committee of the Communist Party of the Soviet Union)," *Sakharov Speaks*, edited by Andrei D. Sakharov. New York: Alfred A. Knopf, 1974.

low dissidents physicist Valentin F. Turchin and historian Roy A. Medvedev, maintains that the only way for the Soviet Union to advance and keep pace with the West is by allowing many different voices to be heard through legal dissent. Freedom of speech and the ability to criticize government policy are essential, Sakharov argues, to provide the necessary variety needed in problem solving and technological advancement.

At the present time it is urgently necessary to carry out a series of measures directed toward the further democratization of public life in the country. This necessity arises from the existence of a close link between the problems of technical-economic progress and scientific methods of management, on the one hand, and questions of information, publicity, and competition on the other. This necessity arises also from other internal and external political problems.

To Strengthen Socialism

Democratization must facilitate the maintenance and strengthening of the Soviet socialist system, of the socialist economic structure, of our social and cultural achievements and socialist ideology.

Democratization carried out under the direction of the CPSU [Communist Party of the Soviet Union] in cooperation with all levels of society should preserve and strengthen the leading role of the Party in the economic, political, and cultural life of society.

Democratization must be gradual in order to avoid possible complications and disruptions. At the same time, it must be profound and it must be carried out consistently and on the basis of carefully worked-out programs. Without deep-rooted democratization, our society will not be able to solve the problems it faces and will not be able to develop normally. . . .

Anti-Democratic Distortions

What is the matter? Why didn't we become the trailblazers of the second industrial revolution? Why couldn't we at least stay even with the most developed capitalist countries? Is it really true that the socialist system provides poorer possibilities than the capitalist for the development of productive force and that in economic competition socialism can't beat capitalism?

Of course not! The source of our difficulties is not in the socialist system. On the contrary, it lies in those qualities and conditions of our life that run counter to socialism and are hostile to it. Their cause—anti-democratic traditions and norms of public life—arose during the Stalin period[1] and has not been completely liquidated to this day. Economic constraints, limitations on the exchange of information, restrictions of intellectual freedom, and other anti-democratic distortions of socialism that took place in Stalin's time are still accepted as a kind of necessary cost of the process of industrialization. . . .

Exchange of Information Is Needed

Due to the increase in the size and complexity of economic systems, problems of organization and management have taken first place. These problems cannot be solved by one individual or even several individuals who possess power and who "know all." They demand the creative participation of millions of people on all levels of the economic system. They demand a wide exchange of information, and this is what distinguishes contemporary economics from, say, the economics of the countries of the ancient East. But in the process of exchanging information and ideas in our country we face insurmountable difficulties. Negative phenomena and real information about our faults are kept secret because they might be "used for hostile propaganda."

The exchange of information with foreign countries is limited by the fear of "penetration of hostile ideology." Theoretical conceptions and practical proposals that seem somehow too bold are suppressed instantly without discussion, out of fear that they may "destroy the foundations."

One can see clear distrust of creative thinkers, critics, and active personalities. Under these conditions those who advance on the service ladder are not those distinguished by high professional qualities and principles but those who by their words display dedication to the cause of the Party, but who in deeds are distin-

1. the reign of Joseph Stalin, 1924 to 1953

guished only by dedication to their own narrow personal interests or by passive performance.

Restrictions on freedom of information not only make difficult any control over the leadership, not only frustrate the people's initiative, but also deprive even those heading middle-level administrations of both rights and information, transforming them into passive bureaucrats. Our leaders receive incomplete and edited information and are prevented from using their power effectively....

Democratization Will Rejuvenate the Country

Most of the intelligentsia and youth realize the necessity of democratization, the need for cautious and gradual approaches in this matter, but they cannot understand or justify actions having a clearly anti-democratic character. Actually, how can one justify the imprisonment, the detention in camps and psychiatric clinics, of persons who are oppositionists but whose opposition is still within legal bounds in the area of ideas and convictions? In a series of cases the matter lies not in some kind of opposition, but in a simple desire for information, for frank, impartial discussion of important social questions!

It is impermissible to keep writers in prison because of their work. One cannot understand or justify such stupid, harmful measures as the expulsion from the Writers Union of the greatest and most popular Soviet writer [Aleksander Solzhenitsyn], nor the destruction of the editorial board of *Novy Mir*, around which gathered the most progressive forces of Marxist-Leninist socialist direction!

One must speak again of ideological problems.

Democratization with full information and competition must return to our ideological life (social science, art, propaganda) its essential dynamism and creative character, liquidating the bureaucratic, ritualistic, dogmatic, official-hypocritical ungifted style that today occupies so important a place.

A policy of democratization would remove the gap between the Party-state apparatus and the intelligentsia. Mutual lack of understanding would be replaced by close cooperation. A policy of democratization would stimulate enthusiasm comparable to that of the 1920's. The best intellectual forces of the country would be mobilized for the solution of social and economic problems.

A Difficult but Essential Task

To carry out democratization is not easy. Its normal progress will be threatened from one side by individualist, anti-socialist forces and from the other side by those worshipers of "strong power," demagogues of a fascist type who may attempt to utilize the economic difficulties of the country for their own aims, and by mutual misunderstanding and mistrust on the part of the intelligentsia and the Party-state apparatus and the existence in some levels of society of bourgeois and nationalist sentiments.

But we must realize that there is no other way out for our country and that this difficult problem must be solved. Democratization at the initiative of, and under the control of, the highest authorities will allow this process to advance gradually and thus to enable all the links of the Party-state apparatus successfully to change over to the new style of work, which, in contrast with the past, will involve greater public information, openness, and wider discussion of all problems.

Viewpoint 6

"It goes without saying that Soviet people condemn views that go against the people's fundamental interests and the prevailing political, ideological and moral norms of our society."

The Soviet Union Cannot Tolerate the Criminal Actions of "Dissenters"

Aleksandr Sukharev, interviewed by V. Aleksandrov

The leadership of the Soviet Union always maintained that its citizens were free to express whatever opinions they held. In reality, those who did speak out against the policies of the Soviet government were commonly persecuted. In this article Aleksandr Sukharev, first deputy minister of justice of the USSR, explains to his interviewer, journalist V. Aleksandrov, that Soviet citizens are not punished for their beliefs or for criticizing the government. However, many so-called "dissenters" go beyond criticism and attempt to undermine the Soviet system. According to Sukharev, people who act against the prevailing order in this manner are nothing more than criminals that are subvert-

Aleksandr Sukharev, interviewed by V. Aleksandrov, "Democratic Freedoms in a Socialist Society," *Izvestiia*, October 27, 1976.

ing and damaging the system. Therefore, he asserts, the government is justified in taking action against these "dissenters."

Q*uestion.* [*V. Aleksandrov*]—The bourgeois states' mass news media, and especially the radio stations that broadcast to the Soviet Union and the other socialist countries, systematically and importunately repeat the allegation that there are no democratic freedoms in socialist society. Furthermore, they allege that Soviet legislation has no norms guaranteeing individual rights and freedoms and that if they have been proclaimed this is strictly for propaganda value. . . .

In this connection I would like to ask you first of all to appraise provocational statements of this kind, and also to comment on certain legislative acts defining the legal status of USSR citizens and to answer a number of questions of interest to our readers.

Answer. [*Aleksandr Sukharev*]—. . . Attacks on the democratic foundations of our society and of Soviet legislation occupy an important place in this subversive work [anti-Soviet propaganda]. Attempts are being made to discredit the norms that safeguard individual rights and freedoms in our country. This is no accident: Questions of democracy have always been at the epicenter of the ideological struggle.

Treatment of "Dissenters"

Q.—One of the favorite theses of bourgeois propaganda boils down to a great deal of verbiage about the legal and extralegal persecution of so-called "dissenters" in the USSR and about their alleged placement in psychiatric hospitals. What can you say on this subject?

A.—The absurdity of such claims is obvious to everyone who is the least bit acquainted with our legislation and juridical practice.

It goes without saying that Soviet people condemn views that go against the people's fundamental interests and the prevailing political, ideological and moral norms of our society. But I want to stress that according to Soviet laws citizens are not held criminally or administratively liable for their beliefs. The Messrs. Propagandists know very well that this is a question not of "dissent" but rather of specific, concrete *actions*. . . .

A crime is recognized to be a dangerous action that infringes on the Soviet social or state system, the socialist economic system, socialist property, an individual or the political, labor, property or other rights of citizens. In certain cases, a socially dangerous act of omission is recognized to be a crime. . . .

The criminal code contains an exhaustive list of precisely described concrete actions that are recognized to be crimes and are punishable as such. I must emphasize that Soviet law does not permit the articles of the criminal code to be interpreted by analogy or extension. . . .

I must add: In the USSR criminal penalties for any crime can be imposed only by a court sentence. As far as the talk about putting "dissenters" in psychiatric hospitals is concerned, this is pure invention from start to finish. . . .

Religious Liberty

Q.—Anti-Sovieteers also frequently claim that in our country people are persecuted for their religious beliefs and that believers are subjected to various forms of oppression, up to and including criminal penalties.

A.—. . . [In accordance with the USSR Constitution], both freedom of belief and freedom of antireligious propaganda are recognized for all citizens. . . .

Needless to say, . . . the activities of associations that, under the guise of conducting religious rites, harm citizens' health (a characteristic of fanatical sects), infringe on their persons or their rights or induce them to abjure socially useful activity or civic duties are being curbed and will continue to be. . . .

Q.—. . . The bourgeois press, radio and television, in their efforts to discredit the Soviet system and the Soviet way of life, readily make use of materials provided by so-called "dissidents.". . . Moreover, they portray matters as though it were impossible in the Soviet Union to publicly criticize state agencies and particular difficulties and shortcomings.

A.—Such claims can be made only by people who either have never held a Soviet newspaper or magazine in their hands or are outright liars. Our Party has always regarded criticism and self-criticism as a necessary prerequisite for further progress and as an important means of mobilizing the masses to carry out the tasks of communist construction. Therefore, in our country all attempts to suppress criticism are subject to severe penalties, up to and including the removal of guilty parties from their posts. . . .

We do not hide our difficulties and shortcomings, either from Soviet citizens or from our foreign guests. Incidentally, objective observers constantly take note of this. . . .

Q.—. . . Our ideological adversaries frequently accuse the Soviet press of badgering certain individuals who attempt to criticize the Soviet system. They claim that such persons are groundlessly accused of certain acts, which compromises them and renders them unable to defend themselves against attacks by the press.

A.—To put it mildly, these insinuations contain a double falsehood: first, the claim that published items against certain renegades are libelous; second, the allegation that USSR citizens are defenseless against false accusations in the press.

As a journalist, you yourself know how carefully the facts are verified for each press item that exposes the criminal actions or slanderous statements of so-called "dissidents." Facts from their biographies are cited only when this may shed some light on the true motives behind the acts done by "dissidents." If the published information does not make the moral character of the aforesaid persons especially attractive, our press can't be blamed for that.

As far as the question of the "defenselessness" of Soviet citizens confronted with unfounded accusations in the press is concerned, that too is pure invention. In accordance with Art. 7 of the Principles of Civil Legislation of the USSR and the Union Republics, "a citizen or organization has the right to demand by court action the refutation of information defaming his (its) honor and dignity if the circulator of this information fails to prove that it accords with the facts." Furthermore, "if this information has been disseminated in the press, and if it does not accord with the facts, it must also be refuted in the press."

Moreover, Arts. 130 and 131 of the Russian Republic Criminal Code and corresponding articles in the other Union republics' criminal codes provide criminal liability for slander and insult, a provision that applies to items appearing in the press.

CHAPTER 4

Why Did the Soviet Union Collapse?

Chapter Preface

The dilemma of how to manage the Soviet system plagued the nation for much of its history. From its establishment through the 1920s, Soviet leaders tinkered with the methods and structures of governance. They experimented with different economic programs and various means of political and legal control. The 1920s saw a variety of policies that seemed to mix capitalism with communism, government control of cultural life with freedom of expression. When Joseph Stalin came to power in the last years of the decade, however, he put an end to the hybrid economic policies, implementing a centrally controlled command system. He also imposed strict Communist Party control over all other aspects of Soviet life, ending open expression and creating a monolithic state structure. Many scholars have labeled Stalin's actions a second revolution. Once in place, however, the Stalinist system became entrenched.

When Stalin died in 1953 the Soviet leadership was caught off guard, unable to continue with the political system that Stalin had constructed and controlled for so long but unaware of how to proceed any differently. On the one hand, it was clear that significant change was necessary, particularly an end to the terror and repression perpetrated by the Stalinist government. On the other, there was still extreme loyalty and dedication to the Marxist-Leninist ideals of socialism and a genuine desire to make that system work.

In the struggle for power that ensued after Stalin's death, Nikita Khrushchev emerged as the new Soviet leader. Khrushchev soon denounced Stalin's excesses in a secret speech to the Central Committee of the Communist Party. He ordered the release of thousands of political prisoners and rehabilitated many who had been persecuted under Stalin. He also embarked on a series of programs aimed at fixing the multitude of problems facing the country. He attempted to improve the economy, including introducing new measures in agriculture and industry. He tried to reform the party in an attempt to end its inefficiency and rigidity but without ending its control over Soviet society. He allowed greater freedom of expression and information but still maintained censorship and party control over publications. Ultimately, most of Khrushchev's efforts failed to revitalize the system, and he was ousted from power in 1964 by conservatives who thought his policies were reckless and dangerous. Despite his failure, Khrushchev and his policies would lay the groundwork for future changes, which would come more than twenty years later under the leadership of Mikhail Gorbachev.

When Gorbachev came to power in the mid-1980s, the country faced numerous problems. Gorbachev understood that the Soviet Union was seriously lagging behind the West in its economic production and standard of living and that significant measures were needed to help the nation catch up. Perhaps more important, fundamental changes were necessary for the security of the Soviet Union. Thus he instituted a program of reforms that included a restructuring (perestroika) of the economy. He began by decentralizing some elements of the economy, thus giving enterprises more ability to control their own production. As stated by historian Peter Kenez, "He wanted to combine what seemed to him the best in socialism . . . with the undoubted efficiency of the market." Yet he soon realized that these efforts would fail without supporting measures in society, particularly the free and open flow and exchange of ideas and information. As a result, he introduced a policy of openness (glasnost).

Although Gorbachev's reforms included elements of capitalism, he remained a dedicated Socialist. He had no desire to transform the Soviet Union into a free-market system. But Gorbachev's reforms could not save the system, which was falling apart due to numerous internal contradictions. Due to his ideological commitment to socialism, most of his changes were halfway measures that usually created more problems than they resolved. His economic tinkering caused inflation and high prices for basic food items such as bread. These high prices, as well as other measures, such as restricting the sale of vodka, caused much resentment among the population. Although his intention had been to shore up and revitalize the ailing Socialist system, in effect his measures further discredited it in the eyes of the Soviet population. To complicate matters, the open discussion fostered by glasnost led to vocal discontent and rebellion on the part of the non-Russian republics. The union began to break apart at its peripheries, and the final collapse was thus inevitable. As Kenez states, "It is almost certain that the disintegration of the union, the further deterioration of the economy, the demise of the old political system would have occurred in any case. No force could have stopped the centrifugal tendencies, and no one had a recipe for a quick and painless recovery of the economy." In August 1991, Gorbachev resigned from his position of general secretary of the Communist Party. One by one, the republics of the union declared their independence. On December 25, Gorbachev resigned as president of the Soviet Union, and on the following day the union formally dissolved.

Viewpoint 1

"This fundamental change of direction is necessary, since we simply have no other way."

Perestroika and Glasnost Are Necessary to Solve the Problems of the Soviet Union

Mikhail Gorbachev

When Mikhail Gorbachev became general secretary of the Communist Party of the Soviet Union in 1985, he recognized that despite its many achievements, the country lagged behind the West in many ways, especially in terms of economics and technology. Therefore, he decided to embark the nation on a program of broad reform. He attempted to revitalize the Soviet economy through his policy of perestroika (restructuring) in order to make it more productive, to free it from the cumbersome bureaucracy of the governmental system, and to improve the quality of life of the average citizen of the USSR. Restructuring involved not only technical and material changes but also an attempt to end corruption, poor morale, cynicism, and apathy.

Mikhail Gorbachev, "Gorbachev and Reform," *A Documentary History of Communism in Russia: From Lenin to Gorbachev,* edited by Robert V. Daniels. Hanover, NH: University Press of New England, 1993.

Gorbachev understood that these far-reaching reforms would not succeed unless Soviet society became open and more democratic. Thus, he proposed glasnost (openness), which included greater (but not complete) freedom of speech, press, association, and criticism. These reforms, he asserted, were necessary not only to advance the Soviet Union, but also to ensure its survival as a great power in the world. The following viewpoint is excerpted from Gorbachev's 1987 report to the plenary session of the Communist Party's Central Committee. Gorbachev assesses the progress of his reform efforts and calls for a renewed commitment to his goal of revitalizing the nation's economic, social, and moral strength.

The April [1985] plenary session and the 27th Party Congress opened the way for an objective critical analysis of the current situation in society and adopted decisions of historic importance for the country's future. We have irrevocably begun restructuring and have taken the first steps on this path. . . .

At the same time, we see that changes for the better are taking place slowly, that the task of restructuring has turned out to be more difficult than it had seemed to us earlier, and that the causes of the problems that have accumulated in society are more deep-rooted than we had thought. The more deeply we go into restructuring work, the clearer its scale and importance become; more and more new unsolved problems inherited from the past are coming to light. . . .

Loss of Momentum

At a certain stage the country began to lose momentum, difficulties and unsolved problems began to pile up, and stagnation and other phenomena alien to socialism appeared. All of this had a serious effect on the economy and on the social and spiritual spheres.

Of course, comrades, the country's development did not stop. Tens of millions of Soviet people worked honestly, and many Party organizations and our cadres acted vigorously, in the interests of the people. All this restrained the growth of negative processes, but it could not prevent them. In the economy, and in other spheres as well, the objective need for changes became urgent, but it was not realized in the political and practical activities of the Party and the state.

The Party Is to Blame

What was the reason for this complex and contradictory situation?

The principal cause—and the Politburo considers it necessary to say this with total frankness at the plenary session—was that the CPSU Central Committee and the country's leadership, primarily for subjective reasons, were unable to promptly or fully appreciate the need for changes and the danger of the mounting crisis phenomena in society or to work out a clear-cut line aimed at overcoming them and making fuller use of the possibilities inherent in the socialist system.

Conservative inclinations, inertia, a desire to brush aside everything that didn't fit into habitual patterns and an unwillingness to tackle urgent social and economic questions prevailed in both policy-making and practical activity.

Comrades, the executive bodies of the Party and the state bear the responsibility for all this. . . .

Negative Effects

Comrades, all this had a negative effect on the development of many spheres of the life of society. Take material production. Over the past three five-year plans, the growth rates of national income declined by more than 50%. For most indices, plans had not been fulfilled since the early 1970s. The economy as a whole became unreceptive to innovations and sluggish, the quality of a large part of output no longer met current demands, and disproportions in production became exacerbated. . . .

We have at the same time been unable to fully realize the possibilities of socialism in improving living conditions and the food supply, in organizing transportation, medical service and education and in solving a number of other urgent problems. . . .

The elements of social corrosion that emerged in recent years had a negative effect on society's spiritual temper and imperceptibly sapped the lofty moral values that have always been inherent to our people and in which we take pride—ideological conviction, labor enthusiasm and Soviet patriotism.

The inevitable consequence of this was a falloff in interest in public affairs, manifestations of spiritual emptiness and skepticism, and a decline in the role of moral incentives to labor. The stratum of people, including young people, whose goal in life came down to material well-being and personal gain by any means increased. Their cynical position took on increasingly militant forms, poisoned the minds of those around them, and gave rise to a wave of consumerism. The growth of drunkenness, the spread of drug addiction and the increase in crime became indices of the falloff in social mores.

Instances of a scornful attitude toward laws, hoodwinking, bribetaking and the encouragement of servility and glorification had a pernicious effect on the moral atmosphere in society. Genuine concern for people, their living and working conditions and their social well-being was frequently supplanted by political ingratiation—the mass handing out of awards, titles and bonuses. An atmosphere of all-forgivingness took shape, while exactingness, discipline and responsibility declined. . . .

This was the situation, comrades, in which the question of accelerating the country's social and economic development and restructuring was raised. In essence, what is involved here is a change of direction and measures of a revolutionary nature. We are talking about restructuring and related processes of the thoroughgoing democratization of society, having in mind truly revolutionary and comprehensive transformations in society.

This fundamental change of direction is necessary, since we simply have no other way. We must not retreat, and we have nowhere to retreat to. . . .

What We Mean by Restructuring

Today there is a need to state once again what we mean by restructuring.

Restructuring means resolutely overcoming the processes of stagnation, scrapping the mechanism of retardation, and creating a reliable and effective mechanism of accelerating the social and economic development of Soviet society. The main idea of our strategy is to combine the achievements of the scientific and technological revolution with a planned economy and to set the entire potential of socialism in motion.

Restructuring means reliance on the vital creativity of the masses, the all-round development of democracy and socialist self-government, the encouragement of initiative and independent activity, the strengthening of discipline and order, and the expansion of openness, criticism and self-criticism in all spheres of the life of society; it means respect, raised on high, for the value and worth of the individual.

Restructuring means steadily enhancing the role of intensive factors in the development of the Soviet economy; restoring and developing Leninist principles of democratic centralism in the management of the national economy, introducing economic methods of management everywhere, renouncing the peremptory issuing of orders and administrative fiat, ensuring the changeover of all elements of the economy to the principles of full economic accountability and to new forms of the organization of labor and production, and encouraging innovation and socialist enterprise in every way.

Restructuring means a decisive turn toward science. . . .

In 1985 Mikhail Gorbachev (right) meets with former U.S. president Ronald Reagan (left) in Geneva, Switzerland, a meeting remembered as a turning point in the Cold War.

Restructuring means the priority development of the social sphere and the ever fuller satisfaction of Soviet people's requirements for good working, living, recreational, educational and medical-service conditions. . . .

Restructuring means the energetic elimination from society of distortions of socialist morality, and the consistent implementation of the principles of social justice. . . .

The ultimate aim of restructuring is clear, I think—a thoroughgoing renewal of all aspects of the country's life, the imparting to socialism of the most up-to-date forms of social organization, and the fullest possible disclosure of the humanistic nature of our system in all its decisive aspects—economic, social, political and moral. . . .

Deepening Democracy

On the political level, the matter at hand is deepening democracy in the electoral system and achieving the more effective and more active participation of voters at all stages of preelection and election campaigns. . . .

It is quite natural that questions of expanding inner-Party democracy be examined within the overall context of the future democratization of Soviet society. . . .

There is also a need to give some thought to changing the procedure for the election of secretaries of district, region, city, province and territory Party committees and of Union-republic Communist Party Central Committees. Here comrades suggest that secretaries, including first secretaries, could be elected by secret ballot at plenary sessions of the appropriate Party committees. In the process, the members of the Party committee would have the right to enter any number of candidates on the ballot. This measure ought to significantly enhance the responsibility of secretaries to the Party committees that elected them, give them more confidence in their work, and make it possible to more accurately determine the extent of their prestige.

Needless to say, the Party's statutory principle according to which the decisions of higher agencies are binding on all lower-level Party committees, including decisions on personnel questions, should remain immutable.

In the Politburo's opinion, further democratization should extend to the formation of the Party's central leadership bodies as well. I think this is perfectly logical. Apparently it would be logical to democratize elections of leadership bodies in other public organizations as well. . . .

Developing Openness

In improving the social atmosphere, it is also necessary to continue to develop openness. It is a powerful lever for improving work in all sectors of our construction and an effective form of control by all the people. Excellent confirmation of this is provided by the experience that has been accumulated since the April [1985] plenary session of the Central Committee.

Obviously, the time has come to begin the drafting of legal documents guaranteeing openness. They should ensure maximum openness in the activities of state and public organizations and give working people a real opportunity to express their opinion on any question of the life of society. . . .

There should be clarity on yet another question. We say that Soviet society should have no zones closed to criticism. This is fully applicable to the mass news media, too. . . .

Defining Socialist Democracy

When we talk about the democratization of Soviet society—and this is a fundamental question for us—it is appropriate once again to emphasize the main, defining feature of socialist democracy. What I mean is an organic combination of democracy and discipline, independence and responsibility, and the rights and duties of officials and of every citizen.

Socialist democracy has nothing in common with an "everything goes" attitude, irresponsibility or anarchy. Genuine democracy serves every person, protecting his political and social rights, and at the same time it serves every collective and society as a whole, upholding their interests. . . .

The open selection of people for promotion—from among both Communists and non-Party people—would be in keeping with the tasks of democratization and the enlistment of broad masses of the working people in management.

In this respect, there is also the question of promoting women to leadership positions on a broader scale. At present, many women are working, and working successfully, in Party and state posts, in science, public health, education and culture, in light industry, trade and consumer services. Today the country needs to have them become even more actively involved in managing the economy and culture, on both the Union and the republic level. We have the opportunities for this. All we have to do is give women trust and support. . . .

Needless to say, we cannot limit ourselves today to mere recognition of the mistakes that were made. In order to avoid similar errors in the future, we must draw lessons from the past. . . .

Good Organization, Efficiency, and Assiduity

Impaired discipline and lowered responsibility have put down too deep roots and are still making themselves felt in a painful way. It was criminal irresponsibility and slackness that were the main causes of such tragic events as the accident at the Chernobyl Atomic Power Station, the sinking of the steamship Admiral Nakhimov, and a number of air and railway accidents that entailed loss of life.

We must create everywhere an atmosphere that would rule out every possibility of a repetition of such things. Good organization, efficiency and assiduity should become a law for everyone.

Finally, a highly important demand is lofty morality on the part of our personnel, such human traits as honesty, incorruptibility and modesty. We now know, not only from the past but also from current experience, that we will not be able to accomplish the tasks of restructuring without strengthening the moral health of society. It is not happenstance that today we have been having sharp collisions with negative phenomena in the moral sphere. I have in mind the struggle to eradicate drunkenness, embezzlement, bribe-taking, abuse of office and favoritism. . . .

I want once again to emphasize the idea that the line aimed at democratization and the creation of a new mechanism of administration and economic management opens up the possibility of achieving the correct combination of political leadership by the Party with an active role for state agencies, trade unions and other public organizations.

Improving the Soviets

We have already adopted basic decisions on improving the activity of the soviets in present conditions. These decisions will allow the soviets to prove their worth as genuine bodies of power in their territory. Changes are taking place in the activity of the soviets, but they cannot satisfy us as yet. We all have a stake in getting the soviets to begin working properly, in the spirit of the times, as quickly as possible.

Party committees should firmly adopt a line aimed at enhancing the role of the soviets and not be guilty of unwarranted interference in their affairs, let alone of usurping their functions. It is no less important that the soviets' executives themselves and the soviets' administrative apparatus begin to work at full strength and rid themselves of inertia and the habit of constantly looking over their shoulder and waiting for instructions. Democratic principles in the activity of the soviets and their executive agencies must be strengthened. . . .

We want to transform our country into a model of a highly developed state, into a society of the most advanced economy, the broadest democracy and the most humane and lofty morality, where the working person will feel himself to be a full-fledged proprietor and can enjoy all the benefits of material and spiritual culture, where his children's future will be secure, and where he will possess everything he needs for a full, meaningful life. We want to force even the skeptics to say: Yes, the Bolsheviks can do anything. Yes, the truth is on their side. Yes, socialism is a system that serves man, his social and economic interests and his spiritual elevation.

Viewpoint 2

"'We must be guided by our Marxist-Leninist principles. Comrades, we must not forgo these principles under any pretexts.'"

Perestroika and Glasnost Will Not Solve the Problems of the Soviet Union

Nina Andreeva

When Mikhail Gorbachev introduced the sweeping reforms of perestroika and glasnost, there were many who welcomed the loosening of the Party's grip and the greater democratization of the country. Some even believed that he was not going far enough with his policies of democratization. But others, particularly conservative Communist Party members, opposed these moves, believing they threatened the very fabric of Soviet society and would damage socialism, perhaps irreparably. They criticized Gorbachev for undermining the values and institutions that made the USSR powerful and unified. When the economic reforms began to falter in the late 1980s, these critics lambasted him further. In 1988 a schoolteacher from Leningrad named Nina Andreeva wrote a lengthy letter to the editors of the main

Nina Andreeva, "I Cannot Give Up My Principles," *Sovetskaia Russia*, translated by *Current Digest of the Soviet Press*, March 13, 1988.

party newspaper expressing much displeasure with Gorbachev's measures. This letter became a rallying cry for the conservative opposition to Gorbachev. In it, Andreeva argues that perestroika and glasnost are not good for the Soviet people. She maintains that the new openness and challenges to the Socialist system encourage an overly critical view of Soviet history, particularly of the Stalin period. Gorbachev's policies are weakening society by deemphasizing the continuing importance of class struggle, argues Andreeva. Furthermore, she asserts, they are eroding the fundamental principles of Marxism-Leninism, upon which Soviet society was founded.

I decided to write this letter after a great deal of thought. I am a chemist, and I teach at the Leningrad Soviet Technological Institute in Leningrad. Like many others, I am an adviser for a group of students. In our days, after a period of social apathy and intellectual dependence, students are gradually beginning to be charged with the energy of revolutionary changes. Naturally, debates arise—about the paths of restructuring and its economic and ideological aspects. Openness, candor and the disappearance of zones closed to criticism, as well as emotional fervor in the mass consciousness, especially among young people, are frequently manifested in the posing of problems that, to one extent or another, have been "prompted" by Western radio voices or by those of our compatriots who are not firm in their notions about the essence of socialism. What a wide range of topics is being discussed! A multiparty system, freedom of religious propaganda, leaving the country to live abroad, the right to a broad discussion of sexual problems in the press, the need for the decentralization of the management of culture, the abolition of compulsory military service—Among students, a particularly large number of arguments are about the country's past. . . .

The Unnecessary Disparagement of Our Past

So much has been written and said about the Great Patriotic War and the heroism of those who took part in it. But recently a meeting took place in one of our Technological Institute's student dormitories with Hero of the Soviet Union V.F. Molozev, a retired colonel. One of the things he was asked about was political repressions in the Army. The veteran replied that he had not encountered any repressions, and that many of those who had started off the war with him and seen it through to the end had become major military commanders. Some of the students were disappointed with his answer. The now commonplace subject of repression has become excessively magnified in the perception of some young people, pushing an objective comprehension of the past into the background. Examples of this sort are not rare.

It's very gratifying, of course, that even "technos" [*tekhnari*] have a lively interest in theoretical problems of the social sciences. But too many things have turned up that I cannot accept, that I cannot agree with. The constant harping on "terrorism" "the people's political servility," "uninspired social vegetating," "our spiritual slavery," "universal fear," "the entrenched rule of louts"—It is from these mere threads that the history of the period of the transition to socialism in our country is often woven. Therefore, it comes as no surprise, for example, that in some students nihilistic views are intensifying, and ideological confusion, a dislocation of political reference points and even ideological omnivorousness are appearing. Sometimes one hears assertions that it is time to call to account the Communists who supposedly "dehumanized" the country's life after 1917.

Disorientation

At the February plenary session of the Central Committee, it was emphasized once again that it is urgently necessary for "young people to learn the class vision of the world and gain an understanding of the connection between common human and class interests. This includes an understanding of the class essence of the changes taking place in our country" [as stated by Ye.K. Ligachev]. This vision of history and the present day is incompatible with political anecdotes, base gossip and the highly dramatic fantasies that one can frequently encounter today.

I read and reread the much-talked-about articles. What, for example, can they give young people except disorientation and revelations "about the counterrevolution in the USSR at the beginning of the 1930s" and about Stalin's "guilt" for the coming to power of fascism and Hitler in Germany? Or a public "counting" of the number of "Stalinists" in various generations and social groups?

We are Leningraders, so it was with special interest that we recently viewed the excellent documentary film about S.M. Kirov. But the text accompanying the shots at some points not only diverged from the film-document but also gave it a certain ambiguity. For example, shots in the film show an explosion of enthusiasm and joie de vivre and the elan of people who were building socialism, while the narrator's text speaks of repression and lack of information. . . .

The Excessive Criticism of Stalin

In talking with students and pondering crucial problems with them, I automatically come to the conclusion that a good many distortions and one-sided views have piled up in our country, notions that obviously need to be corrected. I want to devote special attention to some of these things.

Take the question of the place of J.V. Stalin in our country's history. It is with his name that the entire obsession with critical attacks is associated, an obsession that, in my opinion, has to do not so much with the historical personality itself as with the whole extremely complex transitional era—an era linked with the unparalleled exploit of an entire generation of Soviet people who today are gradually retiring from active labor, political and public activity. Industrialization, collectivization and the cultural revolution, which brought our country into the ranks of the great world powers, are being forcibly squeezed into the "personality cult" formula. All these things are being questioned. Things have reached a point at which insistent demands for "repentance" are being made on "Stalinists" (and one can assign to their number whomever one wishes). Praise is being lavished on novels and films that lynch the era of tempestuous changes, which is presented as a "tragedy of peoples."

Let me note at the outset that neither I nor the members of my family have any relationship to Stalin or his entourage, retainers or extollers. My father was a worker in the Leningrad port, and my mother was a mechanic at the Kirov Plant. My older brother worked there, too. He, my father and my sister were killed in battles against the Hitlerites. One of my relatives was repressed and was rehabilitated after the 20th Party Congress. Together with all Soviet people, I share the anger and indignation over the large-scale repressions that took place in the 1930s and 1940s through the fault of the Party and state leadership of that time. But common sense resolutely protests the monochromatic coloring of contradictory events that has now begun to prevail in certain press organs.

I support the Party's call to uphold the honor and dignity of the trailblazers of socialism. I think that it is from these Party and class positions that we should assess the historical role of all Party and state leaders, including Stalin. In this case, one must not reduce the matter to the "court" aspect or to abstract moralizing by people far removed from that stormy time and from the people who lived and worked then. Indeed, they worked in such a way that what they did is an inspirational example for us even today.

The Positive Role of Stalin

For me and for many other people, the decisive role in assessing Stalin is played by the firsthand testimony of contemporaries who came into direct contact with him, on both our side of the barricades and the other side. Those in the latter group are not without interest. For example, take Churchill, who in 1919 was proud of his personal contribution to organizing the military intervention of 14 foreign states against the young Soviet Republic but who, exactly 40 years later, was forced to use the following words to characterize Stalin—one of his most formidable political opponents:

"He was a man of outstanding personality who left an impression on our harsh times, the period in which his life ran its course. Stalin was a man of extraordinary energy, erudition and inflexible will, blunt, tough and merciless in both action and conversation, whom even I, reared in the British Parliament, was at a loss to counter. His works resounded with gigantic strength. This strength was so great in Stalin that he seemed unique among leaders of all times and peoples. . . . This was a man who used his enemies' hands to destroy his enemy, who made us, whom he openly called imperialists, do battle against imperialists. He found Russia with a wooden plow, but he left it equipped with atomic weapons." This assessment and admission on the part of a faithful guardian of the British Empire cannot be attributed to dissimulation or political expediency.

The basic elements of this characterization can also be found in the memoirs of [French leader Charles] De Gaulle and in the reminiscences and correspondence of other European and American political figures who dealt with Stalin, both as a wartime ally and as a class adversary. . . .

From long and frank discussions with young people, we draw the conclusion that the attacks on the state of the dictatorship of the proletariat and on the leaders of our country at that time have not only political, ideological and moral causes but also their own social substratum. There are quite a few people who have a stake in broadening the staging area of these attacks, and not just on the other side of our borders. Along with the professional anticommunists in the West, who long ago chose the supposedly democratic slogan of "anti-Stalinism," there live and thrive the descendants of the classes overthrown by the October Revolution, by no means all of whom have been able to forget the material and social losses of their forebears. . . .

An Unambiguous Assessment

As is known, any historical figure is shaped by specific social, economic, ideological and political conditions, which have a determining influence on the subjective and objective selection of aspirants who are called upon to solve various social problems. Having come to the forefront of history, such an aspirant, in order to "remain afloat" must satisfy the requirements of the era and of the leading social and political structures and must realize an objective pattern in his activity, inevitably leaving the "imprint" of his personality on historical events. In the final analysis, for example, few people today are disturbed by the personal qualities of Peter the Great, but everyone remembers that the country rose to the level of a great European power during this rule. Time has condensed the result that is now contained in our assessment of the historical personality of the Emperor Peter. And the ever-present flowers on his sarcophagus in the cathedral of the Peter and Paul Fortress embody the respect and gratitude of our contemporaries, who are far removed from the autocracy.

I think that, no matter how contradictory and complex a given figure in Soviet history may be, his true role in the construction and defense of socialism will, sooner or later, receive an objective and unambiguous assessment. Needless to say, it will be unambiguous not in the sense of being one-sided, of whitewashing or eclectically summing up contradictory phenomena, of an assessment that makes it possible, with qualifications, to create any kind of subjectivism, to "forgive or not forgive," to "discard or keep" elements of history. An unambiguous assessment means above all a historically concrete, nonopportunistic assessment that manifests—in terms of historical result!—the dialectics of the conformity of a given individual's activity to the basic laws of the development of society. In our country, these laws were also connected with the resolution of the question "Who will win?," in its domestic and international aspects. If we are to follow the Marxist-Leninist methodology of historical research, then we must first of all, in M.S. Gorbachev's words, vividly show how millions of people lived, how they worked and what they believed in, and how victories and setbacks, discoveries and mistakes, the radiant and the tragic, the revolutionary enthusiasm of the masses and violations of socialist legality, and sometimes even crimes, were combined.

For me, there is no doubt that, in the question of assessing Stalin's activity, the Party Central Committee's resolution on overcoming the personality cult and its effects, adopted in 1956, and the report of the General Secretary of the CPSU Central Committee devoted to the 70th anniversary of the Great October Socialist Revolution remain the scientific guidelines to this day.

The Attack on Class Struggle

Recently, one of my students startled me with the revelation that the class struggle is supposedly an obsolete concept, as is the leading role of the proletariat. It would be all right if she were the only one maintaining such a thing. But, for example, a furious argument broke out recently over a respected academician's assertion that the present relations between states of the two different social and economic systems are devoid of class content. I admit that the academician did not deem it necessary to explain why for several decades he had written the exact opposite—that peaceful coexistence is nothing other than a form of class struggle in the international arena. It turns out that the philosopher has now repudiated that notion. Well, views do change. However, it seems to me that the duty of a leading philosopher does enjoin him to explain, at least to those who have learned and are learning from his books. What—does the international working class today, in the form of its state and political organs, really no longer act as a countervailing force to world capital?

It seems to me that the same question—which class or stratum of society is the guiding and mobilizing force of restructuring?—is at the center of many current debates. This was talked about, among other things, in an interview with the writer A. Prokhanov in our city newspaper *Leningradsky rabochy* [Leningrad Worker]. Prokhanov proceeds from the premise that the special nature of the present state of social consciousness is characterized by the existence of two ideological currents or, as he says, "alternative towers" that are trying, from different directions, to overcome the "socialism that has been built in battle" in our country. While he exaggerates the significance and acuteness of the mutual confrontation between these "towers," the writer nevertheless rightly emphasizes that "they agree only on exterminating socialist values." But both, their ideologists assure us, are "in favor of restructuring."

The first, and deepest, ideological current that has already revealed itself in the course of restructuring claims to be a model of some kind of left-liberal dilettantish socialism, to be the exponent of a humanism that is very true and "clean" from class incrustations. Against proletarian collectivism, the adherents of this current put up "the intrinsic worth of the individual"—with modernistic quests in the field of culture, God-seeking tendencies, technocratic idols, the preaching of the "democratic" charms of present-day capitalism and fawning over its achievements, real and imagined. Its representatives assert that we have built the wrong kind of socialism and that only today, "for the first time in history, has an alliance come about between the political leadership and the progressive intelligentsia." At a time when millions of people on our planet are dying from hunger, epidemics and imperialism's military adventures, they demand the immediate drafting of a "legal code for the protection of animal rights," ascribe a singular, supernatural intelligence to nature, and claim that cultivation is not a social but a biological quality, transmitted genetically from parents to children. Tell me: What does all this mean?

The Dangers of Left-Liberalism

It is the champions of "left-liberal socialism" who are shaping the tendency to falsify the history of socialism. They suggest to us that in the country's past only the mistakes and crimes are real, in doing so keeping quiet about the supreme achievements of the past and the present. Laying claim to complete historical truth, they substitute scholastic ethical categories for social and political criteria of the development of society. I would very much like to understand: Who needs, and why, to have every prominent leader of the Party Central Committee and the Soviet government compromised after he leaves office and discredited in connection with his actual or supposed mistakes and miscalculations, made while solving some very complex problems on roads uncharted by history? Where did we get this passion for squandering the prestige and dignity of the leaders of the world's first socialist country?

Another special feature of the views of the "left-liberals" is an obvious or camouflaged cosmopolitan tendency, a sort of nationality-less "internationalism." I have read somewhere that when, after the Revolution, a delegation of merchants and factory owners came to the Petrograd Soviet to see Trotsky "as a Jew" complaining of oppression by Red Guards, he declared that he was "not a Jew but an internationalist," which thoroughly bewildered the supplicants.

For Trotsky, the concept of the "national" meant a kind of inferiority and narrowness in comparison to the "international." That's why he emphasized the "national tradition" of October, wrote about "the national element in Lenin," maintained that the Russian people "had received no cultural legacy," etc. For some reason, we are ashamed to say that it was the Russian proletariat, which the Trotskyists slighted as "backward and uncultured" that carried out, in Lenin's words, "the three Russian Revolutions," or that the Slavic peoples were in the vanguard of mankind's battle against fascism. . . .

Here is something else that alarms me: Militant cosmopolitanism is now linked with the practice of "refusenikism"—of "refusing" socialism. Unfortunately, we suddenly think of this only when its neophytes plague us with their outrages in front of Smolny or under the Kremlin's walls. Moreover, we are somehow gradually being trained to see this phenomenon as an almost inoffensive change of "place of residence," not as class and nationality betrayal by persons most of whom have been graduated from higher schools and graduate schools at public expense. In general, some people are inclined to look at "refusenikism" as some kind of manifestation of "democracy" and "human rights," feeling that the talents of those involved have been prevented from blossoming by "stagnant socialism." Well, if over there, in the "free world" their tireless enterprise and "genius" aren't appreciated and selling their conscience doesn't interest the special services, they can come back—. . .

Whereas the "neoliberals" are oriented toward the West, the other "alternative tower" . . . , the "guardians and traditionalists," seeks to "overcome socialism by moving backward"—in other words, to return to the social forms of presocialist Russia. The spokesmen for this unique "peasant socialism" are fascinated with this image. In their opinion, a loss of the moral values that the peasant community had accumulated through the dim haze of centuries took place 100 years ago. The "traditionalists" have rendered undoubted services in exposing corruption, in fairly solving ecological problems, in combating alcoholism, in protecting historical monuments and in countering the dominance of mass culture, which they rightly assess as a psychosis of consumerism.

At the same time, the views of the ideologists of "peasant socialism" contain a misunderstanding of the historical significance of October for the fatherland's fate, a one-sided appraisal of collectivization as "frightful arbitrary treatment of the peasantry," uncritical views on religious-mystical Russian philosophy, old tsarist concepts in scholarship relating to our country's history, and an unwillingness to see the postrevolutionary stratification of the peasantry and the revolutionary role of the working class.

In the class struggle in the countryside, for example, there is frequently an overemphasis on "village" commissars who "shot middle peasants in the back." There were, of course, all kinds of commissars in our enormous country, which had been stirred to new life by the Revolution. But the basic tenor of our life was determined by those commissars who were themselves shot. It was they who had stars cut into their backs or were burned alive. The "attacking class" had to pay not only with the lives of commissars, Chekists [state security personnel], village Bolsheviks, members of poor peasants' committees and "twenty-thousanders" [industrial workers who helped in the collectivization of agriculture in the early 1930s—Trans.], but also those of the first tractor drivers, rural correspondents, girl-teachers and rural Young Communists, with the lives of tens of thousands of other unknown fighters for socialism.

Remain True to Marxism-Leninism

The difficulties in the upbringing of young people are deepened still more by the fact that unofficial [*neformalny*] organizations and associations are being created in the pattern of the ideas of the "neo-liberals" and "neo-Slavophiles." In some cases, extremist elements capable of provocations are gaining the upper hand in the leadership of these groups. Recently, the politicization of these grass-roots [*samodeyatelny*] organizations on the basis of a pluralism that is far from socialist has been noted. Frequently the leaders of these organizations talk about "power-sharing" on the basis of a "parliamentary regime," "free trade unions," "autonomous publishing houses," etc. In my opinion, all this makes it possible to draw the conclusion that the main and cardinal question in the debates now under way in the country is the question of recognizing or not recognizing the leading role of the Party and the working class in socialist construction, and hence in restructuring—needless to say, with all the theoretical and practical conclusions for politics, the economy and ideology that stem therefrom. . . .

Today, the question of the role and place of socialist ideology has taken on a very acute form. Under the aegis of a moral and spiritual "cleansing" the authors of opportunistic constructs are eroding the boundaries and criteria of scientific ideology, manipulating openness, and propagating an extrasocialist pluralism, which objectively impedes restructuring in social consciousness. This is having an especially detrimental effect on young people, something that, I repeat, we higher-school instructors, schoolteachers and all those who deal with young people's problems are distinctly aware of. As M.S. Gorbachev said at the February plenary session of the CPSU Central Committee: "In the spiritual sphere as well, and perhaps in this sphere first of all, we must be guided by our Marxist-Leninist principles. Comrades, we must not forgo these principles under any pretexts."

We stand on this, and we will continue to do so. We have not received these principles as a gift: We have gained them through suffering at decisive turning points in the history of the fatherland.

Viewpoint 3

"The explosion of national feeling . . . was one of the unplanned consequences of perestroika."

The Collapse of the Soviet Union Was a Revolution from Below

Peter J.S. Duncan

Peter J.S. Duncan is a professor in the Department of Social Sciences, School of Slavonic and East European Studies at University College, London. In this viewpoint he explains the fall of the Soviet state as a result of the forces unleashed by Mikhail Gorbachev through perestroika and glasnost. Although these policies were intended to revitalize the Communist system, the freedoms and open flow of information they allowed caused a wave of democratic thought and action throughout the Soviet Union. People began to openly discuss matters of government and public policy, centralized control of the governmental apparatus was loosened, and political groups other than the Communist Party were legalized and allowed to participate in elections. The upsurge of nationalism experienced by the populations of the non-Russian republics, especially the Baltic states of Latvia, Lithuania, and

Peter J.S. Duncan, "The Democratic Transition in Russia: From Coup to Referendum," *Parliamentary Affairs*, vol. 46, October 1993, pp. 491–504. Copyright © 1993 by Oxford University Press. Reproduced by permission.

Estonia, put pressure upon the central government in Moscow for independence and therefore also contributed to the collapse. The people of the Soviet Union responded to their new freedom by organizing political resistance to the Communists and ultimately voted them out of power. Thus, Duncan paints a portrait of a popular democratic revolt by the citizenry of the USSR.

In Russia, democratization has been a long, complex and incomplete process which began in the last years of the existence of the Soviet Union and has continued, since the dissolution of the USSR, in the Russian Federation. When Mikhail Gorbachev was appointed General Secretary of the Central Committee of the Communist Party of the Soviet Union in March 1985, the USSR was facing a serious economic and social crisis, with zero growth and widespread corruption. Political dissent had been virtually extinguished over the previous five years, with a neo-Stalinist cloud of repression hanging over the country. The pattern of Communist rule over seventy years in Russia had both been shaped by and tended to reinforce the political tradition of centuries of autocracy.

Gorbachev's early attempts at economic reform ran up against the obstruction of the party and state bureaucracy, and he concluded that some degree of political reform was essential if the USSR was to solve its economic and social problems. He launched the policies of 'glasnost' and 'perestroika' without clearly defining them, or knowing where he was going. Glasnost signified not only openness but also the idea of giving the people and the press their voice, allowing them to criticize the shortcomings of Soviet society. It was a bid for the political support of the intelligentsia for change as well as to explain to society how essential change was. With their attachment to collectivism and egalitarianism, working-class Russians seemed likely to be suspicious of any reform which threatened their job security. Glasnost was boosted by the shock of the Chernobyl nuclear accident. Informal associations were formed to discuss, and act on, issues such as the environment, conservation and the nature of Stalinism. At the January 1987 Plenum of the Central Committee, Gorbachev declared that past attempts to reform the Soviet system had failed because they had not involved the masses. In the course of 1987 and 1988, virtually all the political dissidents were released from prison and labour camps and were allowed to resume their political activity— very often (and contrary to Gorbachev's intentions) of a nation- alist nature.

Perestroika

Perestroika—restructuring—was originally used by Gorbachev with reference to the economy, but he also came to call for pere- stroika of the political system. His strategy was to shift power from the party apparatus to revived and democratized soviets. The rubber-stamp Supreme Soviet, which met for only a few days each year, would be replaced by a standing parliament. He faced intense opposition, not only in the apparatus but in the Politburo, the po- litical leadership of the party, which remained dominated by con- servatives. . . .

The amendments to the Soviet Constitution, passed in late 1988, provided for the election of a new supreme legislative body, the Congress of People's Deputies of the USSR. 1,500 deputies would be elected on the same basis as the old Supreme Soviet, but with competitive elections. A further 750 places were reserved to offi- cial organizations, such as the CPSU [Communist Party of the So- viet Union] and the trade unions. The Congress would meet every year for a few days, and its main task would be to elect from its members the standing parliament, the Supreme Soviet, composed of two equal chambers, the Soviet of the Union and the Soviet of Nationalities, each of 271 members. The process of indirect elec- tion would be another built-in safeguard.

The electoral process revealed yet another means whereby local officials could retain control: pre-election meetings could reject any of the candidates nominated for the seats open for popular election. In practice, this vetting procedure varied from place to place. In the main towns of Russia, informal associations came to- gether to create Popular Fronts or electoral blocs to put up their own candidates or to campaign for others whom they supported. They hoped to imitate the success of the Popular Fronts in the Baltic republics, which had acquired a mass membership. . . .

Boris Yeltsin's Campaign

It was in Moscow that Boris Yeltsin decided to try to make his political comeback. In November 1987 he had been sacked from his post as party leader of the city and publicly humiliated for criticizing the slow pace of perestroika and personally attacking the most influential conservative on the Politburo, Egor Ligachev. The antagonism between Yeltsin and Gorbachev was a significant factor affecting the pace of the transition to democracy in Russia. Fearing that Yeltsin would win the Moscow seat for which he was standing, the Central Committee announced an enquiry into his activities. The Moscow Popular Front and other radical candidates declared their support for him. This laid the groundwork for the cooperation between the intellectuals of the informal groups and the former CPSU official.

The informal groups campaigned with posters, leaflets and megaphones in support of their candidates. They did not succeed in achieving the mass activity level found in the Baltic republics, but they had to confront a tradition of apathy and scepticism. The result of the elections was a serious defeat for the party apparatus. Yeltsin won 90% of the vote in his constituency, reflecting public support for his stand against corruption and sympathy for his earlier victimization. Several other radicals were elected in Moscow, undoubtedly helped by their association with him. In Leningrad "Elections 89" humiliated the Communist apparatus, defeating six major local figures, including the regional party First Secretary, a candidate member of the central Politburo, who was unopposed, but voters took the advice to "Strike him out!" Certainly, in the rural parts and the smaller cities of Russia, and in Ukraine, Belorussia and Central Asia, the party apparatus maintained a near monopoly of the seats. In the Baltic states and in Georgia, on the other hand, the majority of successful candidates were supporters of the independence of their republics from the USSR.

The explosion of national feeling, like the chaos which developed in the economy, was one of the unplanned consequences of perestroika. Already in 1988, strikes, demonstrations and violence had erupted on a mass scale between the two Transcaucasian republics of Armenia and Azerbaijan. The reason was the desire of the mainly Armenian population of Nagornyi Karabakh, an autonomous region in Azerbaijan, to be united with Armenia. In spring and summer 1989, ethnic violence occurred in Georgia and in Central Asia, including the killing of twenty Georgian nationalist demonstrators in Tbilisi by Soviet security forces and fighting between different Muslim nationalities in Central Asia. In the economy, shortages of food and consumer goods developed, partly because of the disruption caused by ethnic unrest but mainly because of suppressed inflationary pressure and the partial abandonment of central planning. The Law on the State Enterprise, passed in 1987, gave an unprecedented measure of independence to industrial firms but, owing to the failure to liberalize prices, it was not always in the interests of enterprises to produce what was most needed.

Fast-Paced Change

Against this background, the Congress of People's Deputies met from 25 May to 9 June. With Gorbachev in the chair, deputies subjected the whole range of Soviet economic, social, environmental and nationality policies to withering criticism. Frantically all the country watched the proceedings live on television (when they should have been working) or listened to them on the radio in public transport. All the supposed achievements of the regime were questioned. This experience played a major role in removing the fear which had previously been present in much of the Soviet population, inhibiting the public expression of criticism. After the Congress, the new Supreme Soviet began to function for the first time as a standing parliament. Instead of passing legislation on the nod, as before, laws were fiercely debated before being passed. When the Prime Minister, Nikolai Ryzhkov, presented his new government, the committees of the Supreme Soviet insisted on grilling the nominees and in some cases rejecting them.

Power at the centre was, in reality, passing from the party bodies to the Supreme Soviet. In the localities, admittedly, the CPSU committees continued to wield power, seeking to minimize the impact of the unwelcome changes emanating from Moscow. In the summer, miners in Siberia and Ukraine went on strike to protest against poor working conditions, unresponsive management, low wages and the shortages of consumer goods. Additionally, they demanded the abolition of Article 6 of the USSR Constitution, which legitimized the "leading role" of the Communist Party. Within the Supreme Soviet, radical deputies under the leadership of Yeltsin and Academician Andrei Sakharov combined in the Inter-Regional Group. In December, at the Second Congress, Sakharov argued for the abolition of Article 6, but Gorbachev cut off his microphone. The General Secretary could no longer control the pace of development. The leaders of the Inter-Regional Group organized the "Democratic Platform" within the CPSU, advocating that the party should transform itself into a social-democratic party and give up its monopoly. The same people played a key role, together with the local Popular Fronts in the Russian cities, in organizing the "Democratic Russia" electoral bloc to fight in the elections for the Russian Supreme Soviet and local soviets, due in March 1990. In February, two huge demonstrations were held, demanding that a multi-party democracy be allowed. Finally, in March, during the Russian elections, Gorbachev himself persuaded the Congress to change the Constitution, removing the "leading role" of the CPSU and opening the way to the legalization of other parties. . . .

Election Results

The Russian elections of March 1990 were conducted much more fairly than the Union elections the year before. There was, again, a two-tier system, with a Congress of People's Deputies of 1,068 members (900 elected on the basis of equal territorial constituencies, and 168 elected to give some extra representation to the autonomous republics and territories within the Russian Federation). This elected a Supreme Soviet of 252 members, composed of two equal chambers, the Soviet of the Republic and the Soviet of Nationalities. Unlike the USSR Congress, there was no provision for the representation of official organizations. Nor was there any attempt to use the pre-election meetings to prevent undesirable candidates from standing. If no candidate won a majority on the first ballot, the top two candidates proceeded to a second ballot. The elections were not organized on a party basis; most candidates were members of the CPSU but might be endorsed by electoral blocs such as Democratic Russia or the nationalist Bloc of Public-Patriotic Forces.

As in 1989, the democrats won major victories in the cities but the conservative Communists retained control of much of provincial Russia. The democratic electoral blocs easily won control of the city soviets of Moscow and Leningrad. They then had to wage a protracted struggle for control of the local government machinery, which remained in the hands of the Communist nomenklatura [the elite of Soviet society]. In the Russian Federation Congress, Democratic Russia won about one-third of the seats, with conservative Communists and Russian nationalists winning nearly one-third and the other deputies being uncommitted. Of all the deputies, 86% were members of the CPSU. Democratic Russia supported Yeltsin (who had been elected from Sverdlovsk) for the post of chairman of the Supreme Soviet. Gorbachev tried to prevent his election, but after several inconclusive ballots he was able to secure a bare majority of votes by agreeing to include people of diverse viewpoints within the republic's leadership. Ruslan Khasbulatov, a Chechen of moderately reformist views, was chosen as his first deputy. . . .

A Parade of Sovereignties

Elections took place for the Supreme Soviets of the other republics of the USSR. In March, all three Baltic republics elected governments which were committed to independence. Lithuania was the first to pass a declaration of independence and to suffer a blockade imposed on Gorbachev's orders. But now Russia, comprising three-quarters of the territory of the Soviet Union, was confronting the central leadership. In July the Supreme Soviet of Ukraine passed a similar declaration of sovereignty. There, although the nationalist forces were in a minority, the Communist deputies reflected the public pressure for more independence. A "parade of sovereignties" followed: not only the Union republics of the USSR but the nationality territories inside the Russian Federation, led by Tatarstan, asserted their desire for greater control. Yeltsin initially welcomed even this. Having declared his support for Lithuania's independence, his concern was to build a coalition of the republics against the centre, to bring about a decentralized and democratized Union.

Meanwhile, in Russia, organizations calling themselves political

parties began to proliferate, with the newly-elected deputies play-
ing a leading role. In addition to the Social Democratic Party of
Russia, the Russian Christian Democratic Movement and the
Constitutional Democratic Party, there were many other smaller
groups, typically built around one leader and having almost in-
distinguishable programmes—demanding a multi-party democracy and a market economy. In May 1990 Nikolai Travkin brought
a number of leading figures in the Democratic Platform out of the
CPSU; despairing of the possibility of reforming the party from
within, they created their own Democratic Party of Russia, symp-
tomatically known as "Travkin's party".

In July 1990 the CPSU held its 28th Congress. It had been pre-
dicted that the party would split, with either the democrats or the
conservatives leaving to establish a new party, which might then
create the basis for a viable two-party system. Gorbachev succeeded in persuading the disgruntled delegates to keep him as
General Secretary, remove Ligachev from the leadership and adopt
an eclectic programme with social-democratic influences. There
was no major split: Yeltsin dramatically left the CPSU and was followed by the chairmen of the Moscow and Leningrad city soviets,
Gavriil Popov and Anatoly Sobchak. These were important sym-
bolic steps; their party membership had ceased to have influence
on their activity, but now these key political positions in Russia
were no longer held by Communists. In November most of the
remnants of the Democratic Platform also left the CPSU and
formed the Republican Party of Russia.

Conservatives Fight Back

Meanwhile, alarmed at the threat to the Union posed by democratization and nationalism, the conservatives in the USSR Supreme
Soviet were fighting back. Having established their own deputies'
group, "Soyuz" (Union), they were in a position to dominate the
Supreme Soviet and to influence Gorbachev. Having toyed with the
idea of adopting a 500-day programme for the transition to the
market economy, Gorbachev allowed himself to be convinced that
this would lead to the destruction of the means of central control.
The CPSU, which had created the USSR and held it together, had
lost its leading role. The market would remove the functions of the

central government apparatus holding the economic threads of the country. As a result, Gorbachev formed an alliance with the conservatives, which put back the democratic transition. Foreign Minister Eduard Shevardnadze resigned in December 1990, warning of the danger of a dictatorship. The following month Soviet security forces in Vilnius and Riga tried to topple the elected governments of Lithuania and Latvia, killing several people, but were forced to abandon the attempt because of local resistance and because Gorbachev was not prepared to pursue that course. Nevertheless, he proposed a moratorium on glasnost and had two critical television programmes taken off the air after they tried to give an objective view of events in the Baltic.

In March 1991 Gorbachev held a referendum on the future of the Union, hoping to undercut the appeal of nationalism. Six republics—Estonia, Latvia, Lithuania, Georgia, Armenia and Moldavia—refused to take part, however, indicating how strong separatist sentiment had become already. Substantial majorities in the other republics voted to remain in the Union. In Russia, however, a similar number voted for Yeltsin's proposal to create the post of a directly elected president of the Russian Federation. Ukraine voted to support its Supreme Soviet's declaration of state sovereignty. With strikes breaking out in Russia in support of Yeltsin, and elsewhere in the Union against his own policies, Gorbachev switched tack again and came to an agreement with Yeltsin and the leaders of the eight other republics which had participated in the referendum. This was to include an agreement to draw up a new Unoin Treaty, granting most economic powers to the republics.

On 12 June 1991 Yeltsin won the Russian presidential election, with 57% of the vote in a relatively low-key campaign. He was helped to victory on the first ballot by choosing as his Vice-President Colonel Aleksandr Rutskoi, a hero of the Afghanistan war who had organized a breakaway faction in the Russian Congress of People's Deputies, Communists for Democracy, which had come to Yeltsin's aid in April when he had been under conservative attack. Ryzhkov, the former Soviet Prime Minister, who had the support of the newly-formed Russian section of the Communist Party, came second with 17% of the vote, and Vladimir Zhirinovsky, leader of the extreme right-wing imperialist Liberal-

Democratic Party, came third with 8%. Installed with a popular mandate that Gorbachev had neither sought nor gained, Yeltsin proceeded to dissolve party organizations in economic institutions and threatened to do the same in the Army and KGB.

The Coup and Its Aftermath

The coup of 19–21 August was an attempt by leading conservatives to turn the clock back. The heads of the KGB, the Ministry of Defence and the Ministry of Internal Affairs, the USSR Vice-President, Prime Minister and leaders of the military-industrial complex established the State Committee for the State of Emergency. They arrested Gorbachev and sent troops into Moscow. They aimed to prevent the signing of the new Union Treaty which would have taken away much of their power and, they believed, led to the disintegration of the USSR. But Gorbachev refused to cooperate, while Yeltsin evaded arrest and went to the Russian Supreme Soviet building to organize resistance: the television showed him standing on a tank, declaring the coup illegal. While the majority of the population carried on life as normal, hundreds of thousands of people turned out to demonstrate against the coup. The refusal of the troops to fire on unarmed civilians and the reluctance of the plotters themselves to cause a bloodbath sealed its fate. Gorbachev and the Union institutions were severely weakened by the coup, the Union legislature had to dissolve itself, and Yeltsin emerged the hero: he passed decrees suspending and then banning the Communist Party.

The Baltic states and most of the other republics declared their independence after the failure of the coup, and this time they were able to put their intentions into practice. Attempts to preserve an economic union and to create a new political union, the Union of Sovereign States, persisted until Ukraine voted overwhelmingly for independence on 1 December. Yeltsin, the Ukrainian President Kravchuk and the Belorussian leader Stanislau Shushkevich signed the Minsk agreement on 8 December, terminating the existence of the USSR and forming the Commonwealth of Independent States. This created a framework in which the relations between the former republics of the USSR, including Ukraine, could be handled, while at the same time allowing Yeltsin to remove Gorbachev from office.

Viewpoint 4

"In contrast to the conventional wisdom, the Soviet revolution of 1991 was made, not against the small elite that ran the Soviet Union, but rather by that elite."

The Collapse of the Soviet Union Was a Revolution from Above

David Kotz and Fred Weir

The majority of interpretations of the collapse of the Soviet Union portray the event as a movement by the masses. The Soviet people, tired of the economic stagnation and the political restriction on their lives, removed the Communists from power. David Kotz, a professor of economics at the University of Massachusetts, Amherst, and Fred Weir, a journalist who lives in Russia, present a different view of the fall. Instead of a revolution from below, Kotz and Weir insist that the change came from above. It was the leadership of the Soviet Union that wanted to end the Soviet-style Socialist system and introduce capitalism and the free market. One merely has to examine the new ruling elite of Russia after the end of the Soviet Union; many of the

David Kotz and Fred Weir, "Why Did the USSR Fall? The Party Elite, Not the Masses, Wanted Capitalism," *Dollars & Sense*, July/August 1997. Copyright © 1997 by *Dollars & Sense*, a progressive economics magazine, www.dollars andsense.org. Reproduced by permission.

same Communists who controlled the country prior to 1991 retained a great deal of power and influence after that fateful year. Moreover, as Kotz and Weir assert, many of them greatly benefited from the transition, amassing tremendous wealth through the onset of capitalism. The authors further contend that the reformers pushing for democracy and capitalism during the last years of the Soviet Union won power not as a result of their popularity with the majority of Soviet citizens, but because they had the support of the Communist Party elite.

Conventional wisdom tells us that the remarkable demise of the Soviet Union in 1991 was propelled by the collapse of its socialist economy, leading the citizenry to peacefully sweep aside the nation's Communist leadership and their misbegotten socialist system. Yet, if one inquires into the whereabouts of the allegedly deposed Communist leaders, one finds most of them not languishing in exile, but still in high-level positions in the 15 new nations that emerged from the USSR. Furthermore, most of them are a great deal richer than they were before the Soviet Union's demise. Two years after this odd revolution, 11 of these 15 new nations were headed by former top Communists.

In contrast to the conventional wisdom, the Soviet revolution of 1991 was made, not against the small elite that ran the Soviet Union, but rather by that elite. And it was not a collapse of the USSR's planned economy that drove this process, because no such collapse took place. While the Soviet planned economy encountered serious problems after the mid-1970s, it was far from collapsing at the end of the 1980s. Rather, the Soviet elite dismantled their own system in pursuit of personal enrichment.

Correctly understood, the USSR's downfall was caused by the undemocratic features of its system, not by the failure of economic planning. This interpretation provides hope that a democratic form of socialism would bring about greatly improved living conditions and economic stability for all members of society, not just an elite—whether capitalist or communist.

For a decade after the Russian Revolution of 1917, the Bolsheviks experimented with various forms of economic organization. Not until the end of the 1920s was what came to be called "the Soviet system" put in place. It was characterized by public ownership of nearly all nonagricultural businesses and detailed planning from Moscow of productive activity across the vast country. Many Western socialists decried the extremely centralized and top-down form of economic planning adopted in the Soviet Union and condemned the authoritarian, repressive form of government that accompanied it.

Income differences were much smaller than those in capitalist countries, and every worker was guaranteed a job. But a privileged and insulated "party-state elite" of high-level officials in the ruling Communist Party and the government ran the system and monopolized the best consumer goods. The Soviet system may have had some socialist features, but it was a far cry from the democratic system of popular sovereignty in both economy and government that socialists around the world had long imagined and worked toward. After Soviet dictator Josef Stalin's death in 1953, the brutal and murderous regime he had presided over since the early 1930s evolved into a more moderate form of authoritarianism, but the basic institutions of the system remained unchanged until the Gorbachev reforms of the 1980s.

Despite the crimes perpetrated in its early decades and the continuing departures from the socialist ideal, the Soviet system brought rapid economic progress for some fifty years after its creation in the late 1920s. The transformation from a rural, agricultural economy to an urban, industrialized one—a process taking 30 to 50 years in other countries, was accomplished in only 12 years, during 1928–40.

Some scholars think that Stalin's forced collectivization of the peasantry, the extreme reduction in their living standards, and the brutally authoritarian work relations in industry largely account for the rapid industrialization of 1928–40. But we believe that Stalin's atrocities, rather than speeding economic growth, instead slowed economic progress by provoking passive resistance from the population.

Economic Growth Under Soviet Socialism

It was the Soviet Union's socialist features, not its repressive ones, that deserve credit for the nation's rapid industrialization.

Excluding the period of war and recovery associated with World War II, much of which was fought on Soviet territory, the Soviet gross national product (GNP) grew at a high average rate of 5.1% per year during 1928–75, based on Western estimates (see Table 1). Even during 1950–75, after basic industrialization had been completed, the Soviet economy still grew rapidly—much more rapidly than the U.S. economy during those years, as Table 1 shows.

Table 1: Average Annual Growth Rates of Gross National Product, 1928–1975

Period	USSR	USA
1928–40	5.8%	1.7%
1940–50	2.2%	4.5%
1950–75	4.8%	3.3%
1975–85	1.8%	2.9%

Source: Revolution from Above: The Demise of the Soviet System, Kotz with Weir, Figures 3.1 and 3.2. *Original sources: The Real National Income of Soviet Russia Since 1928*, Abram Bergson, 1961; *Measures of Soviet Gross National Product in 1982 Prices*, Joint Economic Committee, U.S. Congress; others.

The Soviet system had several economic growth advantages over capitalism. These included the ability of economic planners to devote a large part of national output to investment in capital goods and in education and training of the labor force, absence of the periodic recessions that afflict capitalist economies, and the achievement of continuous full employment.

Growth in GNP is an imperfect indicator of economic improvement over time, but other measures confirm the USSR's rapid progress. By 1975 the formerly backward Soviet Union had surpassed the United States in output of crude and rolled steel, cement, metalcutting and metalforming machines, tractors and combines, wheat, hogs, milk, and cotton. In 1960 about half of Soviet families owned a radio, one out of ten a television, and one out of twenty-five a refrigerator; by 1985 there was an average of one of each per family. By 1980 20 million Soviet citizens had college degrees. That same year the USSR had more doctors and hospital beds per capita than the United States, and life expectancy had risen to 69 years, only five years below life expectancy in the

United States. By the 1970s Soviet prowess in science, technology, and economic growth had Western governments worried. Many feared that the future might belong to the Soviet model by virtue of its economic successes, despite its many undesirable features.

Economic Decline

After 1975 Soviet economic growth slowed markedly and its rate of technological advance also declined. By 1985 Soviet leaders knew they had a problem. The U.S. economy had been advancing more rapidly than the Soviet for a decade, a reversal of the past trend. Furthermore, competing with the Reagan administration's military buildup that began in 1981 placed a large burden on the Soviet economy.

Soviet leader Mikhail Gorbachev came to power in 1985 partly due to the Soviet leadership's realization that serious economic reform was required. But Gorbachev's reforms failed to significantly improve the GNP growth rate, which rose only to 2.2% per year during 1985–89 from the previous decade's 1.8% rate (see Table 2).

Table 2: Soviet GNP Growth 1986–1991

Year	GNP Growth Rate
1986	4.1%
1987	1.3%
1988	2.1%
1989	1.5%
1990	−2.4%
1991	−12.8%

Source: Kotz with Weir, Table 5.1. *Original sources: Measures of Soviet Gross National Product in 1982 Prices,* Joint Economic Committee, U.S. Congress; others.

The GNP growth rate in 1975–89, while disappointing compared to the Soviet economy's past performance, was a far cry from economic collapse. The Soviet economy did not experience a single year of falling GNP during 1975–89, while the United States had three such years.

Worsening shortages arose for some consumer goods in the late 1980s, producing long lines at stores. Western observers assumed at the time that this reflected a collapse of production. But the shortages actually resulted from household income rising faster than consumer goods output. The culprit was economic reforms that decentralized control over wages to the individual enterprise level.

In response, household money income, which had been rising by only 3% to 4% per year in the mid 1980s, suddenly rose by 9.1% in 1988 and 12.8% in 1989. With prices fixed by the central planners, cash-flush consumers quickly emptied store shelves, yet real consumption kept rising. While economic performance was lackluster in the 1980s, it was not consistent with the popular view that the Soviet planned economy collapsed.

In 1990 and 1991, however, conditions changed. During those years Gorbachev and the Soviet government gradually lost power to the political movement led by opposition figure Boris Yeltsin. In May 1990 Yeltsin gained control over the Russian Federation, which was then a republic of the Soviet Union. As chief executive of the Russian Republic, Yeltsin was able to gradually seize political and financial power from the Soviet government. In June 1990 Yeltsin persuaded the Russian republic's legislature to declare its sovereignty over all economic resources within the Russian republic. Economic planning was dismantled during this process, and the highly integrated Soviet economy then indeed began to rapidly contract (see Table 2). This contraction, however, was not due to any inevitable "unworkability" of a planned economy; it occurred because economic planning was discontinued, leaving the economy with no effective means of coordination.

The Elite Embraces Capitalism

How was an opposition political movement able to peacefully dismantle the Soviet system, which had faced no effective internal opposition since the 1920s? The answer to this question is found in Gorbachev's efforts to reform the Soviet system, and his efforts' unexpected effects on Soviet society.

Gorbachev and his associates believed that the key flaw in the Soviet system was lack of democracy. They held this responsible both for the serious social and economic problems that had afflicted the Soviet system since the late 1920s and for the relative economic stagnation which had set in after 1975. Restructuring the Soviet system to allow real popular participation, both in the government and in economic decision-making, would, they argued, finally bring out the true potential of a socialist system.

Accordingly, Gorbachev's reform program, known as "perestroika" (reconstruction), had three components. "Glasnost," which meant lifting restrictions on public debate and political organizing, would free the citizenry to participate in public affairs. Democratization of the government, through instituting free elections and eliminating strict Communist Party control over the state, would permit the people to assert sovereignty in the political realm. Economic reforms were aimed at democratizing and decentralizing economic planning. New legislation shifted some power down to the individual enterprise level, where workers were accorded the right to select the enterprise director. The reforms also introduced a limited degree of market control, giving consumers more choices and more was produced.

Glasnost led to a flowering of many different political groups holding various viewpoints about the best future for the Soviet Union. Three positions found the greatest support. One was the leadership's program of building a restructured and democratic socialism. The second was a call to return to the pre-reform authoritarian system. The third was an increasingly open advocacy of abandoning socialism in favor of capitalism.

Winning Over the Party Elite

Glasnost made it possible to advocate viewpoints in opposition to the leadership, and the democratization of Soviet politics made it possible for newly formed opposition groups to legally contend for power. The economic disruptions occasioned by the economic reform efforts tended to undermine public support for Gorbachev and his associates. However, the pro-capitalist grouping, led by Boris Yeltsin, emerged victorious mainly because it won the support of the overwhelming majority of the party-state elite—the most powerful group in Soviet society.

That the party-state elite would opt for capitalism seems at first glance implausible. It is as if the Roman Catholic Church hierarchy suddenly converted to atheism, or the U.S. Chamber of Commerce called for the nationalization of private business. Yet just such a remarkable turnabout took place in the Soviet Union. By the 1980s most members of the Soviet party-state elite—the high officials in the Communist Party, the state, and the system of economic management—had long since ceased to believe the ideology of the system.

As studies by Western Soviet specialists such as Alec Nove, Mervyn Matthews, and Kenneth Farmer discovered, the post–World War II Soviet elite consisted largely of ambitious individuals, lacking any strong personal conviction, who had risen into the elite in search of power, prestige, and material privilege. When in July 1991 one of the authors asked Nikolai L., a longtime member of the Soviet elite, whether he was a member of the Communist Party, he responded, "Of course I am a member of the Communist Party—but I am not a Communist!" As Gorbachev's reforms opened the future direction of the system to debate, the members of this opportunistic elite evaluated the alternatives based on their own interests.

Most of the elite concluded that the democratized socialism advocated by Gorbachev offered no advantages for them. Democratic socialism threatened to eliminate the arbitrary power they had exercised over the citizenry and to reduce their material privileges. The Soviet elite included some genuine believers in the ideals of socialism, including Gorbachev himself, but they turned out to be a small minority.

Some opposition groups called for returning to the pre-reform Soviet system. But surprisingly few members of the elite found this a persuasive position. While the pre-reform system had promoted them into the elite, their material privileges were nevertheless restricted by the socialist pretensions of the old system. They were forbidden to own property or accumulate wealth, and their privileged lifestyle depended entirely on their position in the hierarchy. Displeasing a superior could lead to demotion and loss of the luxuries to which they had become accustomed. When a dozen high-level supporters of the old system tried to pull off a coup in August 1991, it quickly collapsed as the would-be new leaders found almost no support within the Soviet elite for their attempt to reinstitute the old system.

By contrast, capitalism held great appeal for most of the elite.

They noticed how much richer their counterparts in the West were than they, not only absolutely but relative to the average living standard of their country. The Soviet system had enormously valuable assets, and they realized that, if the system were converted to capitalism, they would be the best positioned to become the new owners of these assets.

Newfound Wealth

Indeed, that is just what happened. Russia's Prime Minister since December 1992, Viktor Chernomyrdin, was Minister of Natural Gas in the Soviet days. Today he is believed to be the largest shareholder of the privatized company Gazprom, which controls the Soviet Union's 20% to 35% of the world's natural gas reserves, and appears to be one of the world's wealthiest individuals. One survey found that 62% of the 100 richest businessmen in Russia had previously been members of the Soviet party-state elite (most of the other 38% apparently came from organized crime backgrounds). It also found that 75% of high-level political leaders in President Yeltsin's administration in post-Soviet Russia came from the Soviet elite.

The Soviet elite was not defeated by a democratic revolution from below in 1991. Rather, they remained in power, discarded their Communist identity, and proceeded to divide up the wealth of the Soviet system among themselves.

A study of the Moscow elite in June 1991 by Judith Kullberg, an American political scientist, confirmed that the conversion to capitalism was widespread within the top layer of Soviet society. Of the sample of the elite studied, 77% supported capitalism, 12% democratic socialism, and 10% held a "Communist or Nationalist" position.

The views of ordinary Soviet citizens were vastly different. In May 1991 the Times-Mirror Center for the People and the Press, an American survey research firm, conducted a large-scale public opinion survey in European Russia. It found that, as in the above elite survey, only 10% favored the pre-reform system. But 36% in the public opinion survey favored democratic socialism and another 23% favored the Swedish model of social democracy. Only 17% wanted "capitalism such as found in the United States or Germany" (14% had no opinion). Thus, a large majority (69%) of the public apparently wanted some kind of socialism or social democracy, and few wanted Western-style capitalism. Other public opinion surveys conducted at the time found even less support for capitalism than did the Times-Mirror poll.

But despite the significant democratization of the Soviet system during 1985–91, most ordinary citizens remained politically inactive. The party-state elite, positioned at the pinnacle of the social pyramid, had the power to overcome the resistance of Gorbachev and his associates, despite the public support for Gorbachev's aims, and turn the Soviet Union toward capitalism. Because the leader of the pro-capitalist movement, Boris Yeltsin, won institutional power within the Russian republic, while Gorbachev retained control of the central Soviet state, the pro-capitalist movement's achievement of full state power required dismantling the Soviet state. Such a move had no legal or constitutional basis, and a 1991 referendum found that more than three-fourths of Soviet voters opposed it. Separating Russia from the Soviet Union was the only feasible way for Yeltsin and his movement to pursue a capitalist transformation.

✳ Glossary

"April Theses": Vladimir I. Lenin's policy guidelines issued in April 1917 following the overthrow of the czarist government. It called for a rejection of the provisional government, an end to Russia's involvement in World War I, and transfer of all power to the Soviets.

Bolsheviks: The section of the Russian Social Democratic Labor Party (the Russian Marxists) that split from the main body of the organization in 1903. In October 1917 it was this party that led the revolutionary forces that overtook the government and established the new Soviet system.

Bourgeoisie: The middle class.

Capitalism: An economic system in which ownership of business is held by private individuals who hire workers and pay them wages to produce goods and services for sale on the open market.

central economic planning: A form of economic planning in which the national government maintains control of the entire economy, determining all aspects of management and production. This is the form of economic planning that predominated in the Soviet Union.

constituent assembly: The representative body that was scheduled to be convened in Russia in February 1918 with the goal of creating a new democratic government. The Bolsheviks prevented it from being held once they assumed power in October 1917.

CPSU: Communist Party of the Soviet Union. The only legal political party of the Soviet Union, which maintained control over all aspects of the government, the economy, and cultural and social life in that country.

democratic socialism: An economic and political system in which the workers own the business enterprises and manage them through democratically determined policies.

dictatorship of the proletariat: The stage of Marxist communism

165

in which the working classes maintain control of the apparatus of government and thereby demolish the remnants of bourgeois capitalism.

dissidents: Those individuals in the Soviet Union that expressed dissenting opinions, criticizing the Communist government for its abuse of human rights, its subversion of democratic practices, and its intolerance of alternative opinions.

glasnost: The policy of "openness" introduced by Soviet premier Mikhail Gorbachev in the late 1980s, which included reducing censorship and allowing free discussion of policies, government, and economics with the goal of revitalizing the stagnating Communist system of the Soviet Union.

July Days: A series of street demonstrations and protests that broke out in Petrograd in the early days of July 1917, reflecting growing disappointment with the liberal provisional government and increasing support for the more radical policies of the Bolsheviks, who took the leading role in the demonstrations.

Kornilov Affair: The failed attempt by General Lavr Kornilov, a hero of World War I, to seize power in August 1917 during the turbulent days after the collapse of czarism. It is often interpreted as a counterrevolutionary effort with the goal of establishing authoritarian control.

Mensheviks: The section of the RSDLP that remained after the split with the Bolsheviks in 1903. The Mensheviks favored a more decentralized party structure and did not support the Bolsheviks' bid to seize power in October 1917, arguing that the conditions were premature for a Marxist revolution in Russia.

nomenklatura: The elite of the Communist Party and of Soviet society who enjoyed widespread privileges and benefits unavailable to the majority of the Soviet population, including access to foreign goods, travel, hard currency, elite institutions of higher education, and cultural opportunities.

October Manifesto: The document issued by Czar Nicholas II in October 1905, during a period of revolutionary upheaval culminating in a general labor strike that crippled Russia's economy and forced the czar to make concessions to those advocating reform. The manifesto granted a representative legislature (a parliament) elected on broad suffrage and gave Russia a constitution guaranteeing political and civil rights to its citizens. The effectiveness of the manifesto was severely limited, however, by subsequent measures taken by the czar to curtail the authority and power of the parliament after order was restored.

Okhrana: The czarist secret political police used to suppress dissent and the growing revolutionary movement in Russia during the nineteenth and early twentieth centuries. It was responsible for numerous arrests, exiles, imprisonments, internments in Siberia, and executions of alleged radicals.

perestroika: The policy of "restructuring" introduced by Soviet premier Mikhail Gorbachev in the late 1980s that sought to change the method of economic planning and thereby increase production and overall economic effectiveness. It was later applied to the political system as well, and introduced pluralism.

Petrograd: Capital city of Russia until 1918, previously (and currently) named St. Petersburg, but changed to Petrograd during the First World War due to anti-German sentiment. After Vladimir I. Lenin's death in 1924, the name was changed to Leningrad and remained such until the collapse of communism in 1991.

provisional government: The temporary governing body established immediately after the fall of czarism in March 1917. It represented a coalition of political parties, but the Marxist parties refused to participate in it, labeling it "bourgeois" and contrary to the interests of the working classes they represented. The government was only to exist until the constituent assembly was convened to create a new constitution and government for Russia. It was overthrown by the Bolsheviks in October 1917.

RSDLP: The Russian Social Democratic Labor Party, the Russian Marxist party from which the Bolshevik party, which eventually took control of the Russian government, was spawned.

soviets: Councils of elected representatives created first in 1905 during the revolutionary upheaval to deal with local issues. They came into being again after the fall of czarism in 1917, the most important of which being the Petrograd Soviet of Workers', Peasants', and Soldiers' Deputies, which competed for power with the provisional government. The soviets became the constitutional structure of the Communist state after 1917.

Stalinism: The policies of Soviet leader Joseph Stalin (1929–1953), which focused on heavy and forced industrialization, forced collectivization of agriculture, tight central Communist Party control over all aspects of Soviet life, and widespread purges of alleged "enemies of the people," including mass arrests, deportations, exiles, internments in Siberian labor camps, and executions.

 # For Further Discussion

Chapter 1
1. After reading the platforms of the Union of the Russian People and the Russian Social Democratic Labor Party, which do you think makes a stronger argument for the type of government that is best for Russia? Why?
2. What reasons do Lev Kamenev and Grigori Zinoviev give for postponing the revolution in the summer of 1917? How does Vladimir I. Lenin refute their points?

Chapter 2
1. How does Joseph Stalin support his assertion that Russia can achieve "socialism in one country" despite Leon Trotsky's insistence that, according to the theories of Karl Marx, worldwide revolution is necessary? Why do you think Stalin's theory was more appealing to Soviet Communists?
2. What role does Winston Churchill advocate for the United States in the postwar world? How does this vision compare to that put forth by Nikolai Novikov for the Soviet Union?

Chapter 3
1. The two sources concerning women in the Soviet Union present very different views of their lives. Why do you think the viewpoint from the official Soviet source is so much more positive than the one presented by Hedrick Smith? What aspects of women's lives does each viewpoint focus on? Why does this focus on different aspects lead to different conclusions about women's well-being?
2. According to the viewpoints presented here, does the Soviet definition of freedom differ from that generally understood in the West? How so? What aspects are stressed by the Soviet side and what are stressed by the American side?
3. In making their arguments against dissent, what are the Soviet leaders most concerned about? Do you believe their concerns are legitimate? Why or why not?

Chapter 4

1. What were Nina Andreeva's specific objections to Mikhail Gorbachev's policies? Do you think her arguments were valid? Why or why not?

2. David Kotz and Fred Weir maintain that the collapse of the USSR was essentially a revolution from above. Are they ignoring the role of the population of the country in the process? How so? Compare these arguments about the fall of communism with those in chapter 1 about the revolution of 1917. In what ways were the two events similar? In what ways were they different?

Chronology

1860s–1870s
The revolutionary movement begins to take shape in Russia.

1881
Russian revolutionaries assassinate Czar Alexander II.

1898
The first Russian Marxist party, the Russian Social Democratic Labor Party (RSDLP), is founded.

1903
RSDLP splits over ideological issues into Bolsheviks and Mensheviks.

January 22, 1905
"Bloody Sunday": A peaceful demonstration at the czar's winter palace turns violent when guards fire upon demonstrators.

September 1905
Russia is defeated in the Russo-Japanese War; unrest throughout the country; soviets (councils) of local government are established.

October 1905
The October Manifesto grants constitutional representation.

December 1905
Armed uprisings in Moscow are suppressed.

1914
Outbreak of World War I.

March 8–12, 1917 (February 23–27, old calendar)
The February Revolution: Czar Nicholas II is forced to abdicate and the provisional government is formed.

November 7, 1917 (October 25, old calendar)
The Bolsheviks seize power in Petrograd.

November 8, 1917
Vladimir I. Lenin forms the Soviet government.

December 1917
An armistice with Germany and Austria-Hungary is signed; the Cheka (internal security force) is formed.

January 1918
The constituent assembly is disbanded; separation of church and state is decreed.

May 1918
The Russian civil war begins; Lenin adopts the policy of "War Communism."

July 1918
Adoption of the first Soviet constitution.

1921
The New Economic Policy (NEP) is introduced.

April 1922
Joseph Stalin becomes general secretary of the Communist Party.

May 1922
Lenin suffers his first stroke.

December 1922
Establishment of the Union of Soviet Socialist Republics (USSR).

1923
Lenin's third stroke leaves him largely incapacitated; the triumvirate of Gregory Zinoviev, Lev Kamenev, and Joseph Stalin runs the party and the state for the next two years.

January 1924
Lenin dies.

1926
Leon Trotsky, Kamenev, and Zinoviev struggle for power against Stalin, but are defeated and expelled from the politburo.

January 1928

Stalin reintroduces forcible grain collection.

August 1928

The first five-year plan for industrialization is introduced; beginning of Stalin's "cultural revolution," intended to rid Soviet society of any remnants of "bourgeois" society and the old intelligentsia (to 1931).

Fall 1929

Introduction of mass collectivization and the campaign to eradicate kulaks.

March 1930

Stalin publishes "Dizzy with Success" article, lauding the achievements of collectivization but blaming its problems on local authorities; thousands of peasants withdraw from collective farms.

June 1931

Stalin makes a speech in which he abandons the promise of an egalitarian society.

1931–1932

Soviets sign nonaggression pacts with Poland and France; tensions with Japan increase over Manchuria.

1932

Reintroduction of the internal passport system; party-controlled Union of Writers is created; Stalin announces that the first five-year plan has been completed in four years.

1932–1933

Devastating famines occur in Ukraine, northern Caucasia, and Kazakhstan.

1933

United States recognizes the Soviet Union. The second five-year plan is implemented.

1934

The Soviet Union adopts a policy of collective security and joins the League of Nations; Leningrad party leader Sergei Kirov is murdered (probably on Stalin's orders).

1935

Kamenev and Zinoviev charged with conspiracy in Kirov's murder.

June 1936

An antiabortion law and new family code emphasizing traditional values are passed by Stalin.

August 1936

Show trial of Kamenev, Zinoviev, and fourteen others, who are sentenced to death.

December 1936

Adoption of new "Stalinist" constitution.

July 1938

The third five-year plan is introduced by Stalin.

August 1939

The Soviet Union signs a nonaggression pact with Nazi Germany.

September 1939

Germany invades Poland, sparking World War II; Soviet forces occupy eastern Poland according to the agreement with the Germans.

November 1939

The Soviet Union annexes western Ukraine and Belorussia; the Soviet-Finnish War begins.

August 1940

The Soviet Union annexes Estonia, Latvia, and Lithuania.

April 1941

Stalin ignores warnings of an impending Nazi attack on the Soviet Union.

June 1941
The German invasion (Operation Barbarossa) of the Soviet Union begins.

September 1941
The Siege of Leningrad begins; Kiev falls to Germans.

December 1941
Red Army stops Germans outside of Moscow.

January 1942
The Grand Alliance of Great Britain, United States, and USSR is formed.

September 1942
The Germans attack Stalingrad.

November 1942
The Soviets counterattack at Stalingrad, and the German army is encircled.

February 1943
The Germans are defeated at Stalingrad.

December 1943
The Allies meet at the Tehran conference to discuss the future course of the war.

1943–1945
U.S. lend-lease program supplies aid to the Soviet war effort.

January 1944
The Siege of Leningrad by the Germans is lifted; 1 million inhabitants die during the siege.

February 1945
The Allied conference is held in Yalta, where the future of Europe is discussed; Stalin is given control of Poland in return for promises to enter the Pacific War.

May 1945
World War II ends in Europe when the Germans surrender.

July–August 1945

The Allied conference at Potsdam is held; the Soviet Union declares war on Japan.

September 1945

The end of World War II.

1946

Collectivization is spread to newly annexed territories, and discipline is tightened; Stalin's cultural purges begin; Cold War begins.

September 1947

The Cominform (Communist Information Agency) is established in order to facilitate Communist control of Eastern Europe.

February 1948

The Communists take over the government in Czechoslovakia.

June 1948

The Soviet Union and Yugoslavia break off relations; the Berlin blockade begins.

September 1949

The Soviets test the atomic bomb.

December 1949

The Communists take power in China.

February 1950

The Soviet Union joins in an alliance with China.

June 1950

Beginning of the Korean War.

1951–1955

The fifth five-year plan is implemented.

1952

The Nineteenth Party Congress is held.

March 1953

Stalin dies; he is succeeded by Georgy Malenkov.

July 1953
An armistice is reached in the Korean War; gulag (Siberian labor camps) prisoners revolt.

August 1953
The Soviets test the H-bomb.

September 1953
Nikita Khrushchev becomes party first secretary.

1954
The release of some political prisoners begins, some de-Stalinization begins, and a "thaw" in culture, arts, and literature begins.

May 1955
The Warsaw Pact (an alliance of the Soviet Union and Eastern bloc countries) is formed; the ban on abortion is repealed.

February 1956
Khrushchev delivers his "secret speech" against Stalin's crimes at the Twentieth Party Congress.

October 1956
The "Polish October" and the Hungarian Revolution occur.

November 1956
The Hungarian Revolution is forcibly suppressed by Soviet troops.

1956–1959
The USSR opens to foreign contacts.

February 1957
Khrushchev establishes regional economic councils (*sovnarkhozy*).

June 1957
The antiparty group attempts to unseat Khrushchev.

October 1957
The launch of *Sputnik*, world's first space satellite.

March 1958
Khrushchev becomes premier in addition to first secretary.

October 1958
The Soviets try to force the Allies to hand over Berlin to the East Germans.

September 1959
Khrushchev visits the United States; the rift with China begins.

1959–1965
The seven-year plan of economic development is introduced.

April 1961
The Soviet Union puts the first man in space.

August 1961
The Berlin Wall is constructed.

October 1962
The Cuban missile crisis.

July 1963
The nuclear weapons test ban treaty is signed by the United States and the USSR.

October 1964
Khrushchev is deposed and replaced by conservative Leonid Brezhnev.

1968
The dissident journal *Chronicle of Current Events* appears; the "Prague Spring" introduces reforms in Czechoslovakia.

August 1968
Soviet troops invade Czechoslovakia to end the reforms.

September 1968
The Brezhnev Doctrine is imposed, giving Moscow the right to intervene in any Warsaw Pact country.

1970
Aleksandr Solzhenitsyn wins the Nobel Prize for Literature.

1972

The United States and the USSR sign the ABM and SALT I treaties.

May 1972

President Nixon visits the Soviet Union.

June 1972

The four-power agreement divides Berlin between the United States, Great Britain, France, and the Soviet Union.

1974

The publication of the *Gulag Archipelago* leads to the expulsion of Solzhenitsyn, its author, from the USSR.

August 1975

The Helsinki Accords are signed, guaranteeing human rights and détente between East and West.

October 1975

Soviet physicist and dissident Andrei Sakharov wins the Nobel Peace Prize.

1976

Brezhnev suffers a stroke but continues to rule; dissidents form "Helsinki Watch" committees to monitor human rights abuses in the USSR.

June 1977

A revised constitution is adopted.

1978

Soviet influence begins in Ethiopia, Somalia, and Angola; protests in Georgia to maintain use of Georgian language occur.

1979

The Soviet army invades Afghanistan, ostensibly to aid Communist rebels.

January 1980

Sakharov is exiled to the city of Gorky and put under house arrest; the solidarity movement in Poland begins; the United

States boycotts the Olympic games in Moscow and embargoes Soviet grain in protest over the invasion of Afghanistan.

1981
President Reagan labels the USSR the "evil empire."

December 1981
Polish Solidarity movement is crushed and martial law is imposed.

November 1982
Brezhnev dies and is succeeded by Yuri Andropov.

February 1984
Andropov dies and is succeeded by Konstantin Chernenko.

March 1985
Chernenko dies and is succeeded by Mikhail Gorbachev.

May 1985
Gorbachev introduces an antialcohol program and arms control proposals.

November 1985
First meeting between Reagan and Gorbachev occurs in Geneva.

1986
Perestroika (restructuring) is introduced; "new thinking" in foreign policy is implemented.

April 1986
The Chernobyl nuclear disaster occurs.

Summer 1986
The beginning of glasnost (openness).

October 1986
Reagan and Gorbachev hold a second summit, in Iceland.

December 1986
Sakharov is allowed to return to Moscow; ethnic riots occur in Kazakhstan.

June 1987

Protests against Soviet rule in Latvia occur and spread to the other Baltic states.

December 1987

The United States and the USSR agree to ban intermediate-range nuclear missiles; Gorbachev launches "market socialism" and urges democratization of Soviet institutions; informal citizens groups are formed.

April 1988

Gorbachev announces the intention of withdrawing Soviet troops from Afghanistan.

December 1988

Gorbachev addresses the UN with a non-Marxist speech.

1989

Jewish emigration from the USSR is allowed; demonstrations in the Baltics recur.

February 1989

The last Soviet troops withdraw from Afghanistan.

March 1989

First competitive elections for the national assembly are held.

April 1989

Bloody suppression of demonstrations in Georgia occur.

August 1989

The Communists are voted out of office in Poland.

☀ For Further Research

Books

Academy of Sciences of the USSR Institute of History, *A Short History of the USSR*. Moscow: Progress, 1965.

James Bunyan and H.H. Fisher, *The Bolshevik Revolution, 1917–1918: Documents and Materials*. Palo Alto, CA: Stanford University Press, 1934.

Robert V. Daniels, ed., *A Documentary History of Communism in Russia: From Lenin to Gorbachev*. Hanover, NH: University Press of New England, 1993.

Basil Dmytryshyn, ed., *Imperial Russia: A Sourcebook, 1700–1917*. 2nd ed. Hinsdale, IL: Dryden, 1974.

M.K. Dziewanowski, *A History of Soviet Russia and Its Aftermath*. 5th ed. Upper Saddle River, NJ: Prentice-Hall, 1997.

Orlando Figes, *A People's Tragedy: A History of the Russian Revolution*. New York: Viking, 1997.

Mikhail Heller and Aleksandr Nekrich, *Utopia in Power: A History of the Soviet Union from 1917 to the Present*. New York: Summit, 1982.

Geoffrey Hosking, *The First Socialist Society: A History of the Soviet Union from Within*. Cambridge, MA: Harvard University Press, 1992.

Irving Howe, ed., *The Basic Writings of Trotsky*. New York: Schocken, 1976.

Peter Kenez, *A History of the Soviet Union from the Beginning to the End*. Cambridge: Cambridge University Press, 1999.

Gail Lapidus, *Women in Soviet Society*. Berkeley: University of California Press, 1978.

R. Levering et al., eds., *Debating the Origins of the Cold War: Amer-*

ican and Russian Perspectives. Lanham, MD: Rowman & Littlefield, 2002.

Gordon Livermore and Fred Schulze, *The USSR Today: Perspectives from the Soviet Press.* Columbus, OH: Current Digest of the Soviet Press, 1981.

Roy A. Medvedev, *Let History Judge: The Origin and Consequences of Stalinism.* New York: Columbia University Press, 1989.

Thomas G. Paterson, ed., *The Origins of the Cold War.* 2nd ed. Lexington, MA: D.C. Heath, 1974.

Richard Pipes, *The Three "Whys" of the Russian Revolutions.* New York: Vintage, 1997.

Andrei Sakharov, *Sakharov Speaks.* New York: Alfred A. Knopf, 1974.

Richard Sakwa, ed., *The Rise and Fall of the Soviet Union.* London: Routledge, 1999.

Harry G. Shaffer, *The Soviet System in Theory and Practice.* New York: Meredith, 1965.

Hedrick Smith, *The Russians.* New York: Quadrangle/The New York Times Book Company, 1976.

Ronald Grigor Suny, *The Structure of Soviet History: Essays and Documents.* New York: Oxford University Press, 2003.

John M. Thompson, *A Vision Unfulfilled: Russia and the Soviet Union in the Twentieth Century.* Lexington, MA: D.C. Heath, 1996.

J.N. Westwood, *Endurance and Endeavor: Russian History, 1812–1986.* Oxford: Oxford University Press, 1987.

Women in the Soviet Union. Moscow: Progress, 1970.

Web Sites

History of the Soviet Union, www.uea.ac.uk/his/webcours/russia/ welcome. This Web site is designed to give students speedy access to the rich array of sources on Russian history translated into English and available electronically. Since the collapse of the USSR a host of different organizations, academic and nonacademic, have posted on the Web a mass of valuable documents as well as maps, posters, photographs, and other visual images.

The Library of Congress Country Studies: Russia, http://lcweb2.loc.gov/frd/cs/rutoc.html. A site maintained by the Library of Congress for researchers, covering all aspects of Soviet history and society, including politics, economics, demographics, geography, foreign policy, ethnicity and nationality, religion, climate and environment, migration, arts and literature, and culture.

The Modern Encyclopedia of Russian and Soviet History, www.ai-press.com/MERSH.html. The Modern Encyclopedia of Russian and Soviet History (MERSH) is the most authoritative, comprehensive, and balanced reference work about Russia, the Soviet Union, and Eurasia. It is consulted by scholars, students, librarians, and other researchers worldwide.

Seventeen Moments in Soviet History, www.soviethistory.org/index.php. Directed and created by James von Geldern (Macalester College) and Lewis Siegelbaum (Michigan State University), this site covers some of the most important aspects of Soviet history, including secondary analysis, primary sources, images, and sounds.

Soviet History at Marxists.org, www.marxists.org/history/ussr. Soviet history from the Marxist perspective, covering Soviet politics, society, people, religion, foreign policy, propaganda, military history, and the Communist Party as well as culture, art, music, architecture, and painting. Includes many primary sources and images.

 # Index